Mary Jayne May

10242

If It Please
The King

**Library
Oakland S.U.M.**

PHOENIX FIRST PASTORS COLLEGE
13613 N. Cave Creek Rd.
Phoenix, AZ 85022

Library
Oakland S.U.M.

PHOENIX FIRST PASTORS COLLEGE
13613 N. Cave Creek Rd.

If It Please The King

A Study of the Book of Esther

by
Iverna Tompkins

PHOENIX FIRST PASTORS COLLEGE
13613 N. Cave Creek Rd.
Phoenix, AZ 85022

Iverna Tompkins Ministry, Inc.
Decatur, GA

All Scripture quotations are taken from the King James Version of the Bible.

Photograph by Lt. Col. Theodore R. Cole

IF IT PLEASE THE KING
Copyright ©1983, 1984 by Iverna Tompkins Ministries, Inc.
All rights reserved
Printed in the United States of America
91 90 89 88 87 86 85 84   7 6 5 4 3 2
Library of Congress Catalog Card Number: 83-828-21
International Standard Book Number: 0-9611260-19
Iverna Tompkins Ministries, Inc., Atlanta, Georgia 30034

To Wendy, who periodically stopped typing to re-evaluate herself in her Beloved's presence.

OTHER BOOKS AND BOOKLETS BY IVERNA TOMPKINS

GOD AND I
HOW TO BE HAPPY IN NO MAN'S LAND
HOW TO LIVE WITH KIDS AND ENJOY IT
IF IT PLEASE THE KING
SEVEN STEPS TO WORSHIP *(Booklet)*
THE HOLY AND THE PROFANE *(Booklet)*
THE RAVISHED HEART
THE WAY TO HAPPINESS
THE WORTH OF A WOMAN

FOR INFORMATION ON CASSETTE TAPES, WRITE TO:
WAYS AND PRAISE TAPE LIBRARY
P.O. BOX #711
STAYTON, OR 97383

Contents

PREFACE

The Book of Esther is seldom read by many Christians and reference to it is limited to Mordecai's quote from chapter 4 verse 14, "For such a time as this." Dynamic sermons have been preached from those few words, and as valid as they are, it is a shame that the remainder of this book is left unexplored like an unmined jewel, useless and undiscovered though filled with the potential of unexcelled beauty.

As you study this wonderful and inspired book, may you be encouraged to identify more and more with Esther, who submits herself to be cleansed and prepared to be acceptable to the king. When her desire becomes a reality, she continues in genuine concern for justice, destruction of evil, peace and joy for all who walk according to the king's word.

A life of true submission is not seen in one who submits with some specific goal in mind and returns to self-rule when it is achieved. Rather, as is evidenced in Esther, it is seen in one who entrusts self, family, and possessions in total surrender, motivated by love and faith, to the king; not giving to receive, but giving to please.

The key to this book is, I believe, the key to the message it contains. It is discovered in this not-so-simple statement: "If it please the king." Though implied more often, these words are used six times in the Book of Esther: once by Memucan in presenting a remedy to the situation (1:19); once by Haman in his attempt to secure permission to destroy the Jews (3:9); and four times by Esther, the queen (5:8; 7:3; 8:5; 9:13).

With whom do you identify in saying, "If it please the king"? Might it be with one who tries to find an immediate solution to that which disturbs the king (those who do only what is necessary to relieve present conviction)? Or, as with Haman, in our endeavor to get what we want when we want it, do we just pretend to be concerned about pleasing the king?

"If it please the king" should be the creed of His kingdom. Let us discover how to make it so.

ACKNOWLEDGEMENTS

I have always considered myself a "mouth" rather than a "pen." Consequently, I had no aspirations toward Esther becoming a book.

The encouragement of so many friends who heard the teaching and the transcribing from tapes caused me to consider the possibility of it. However, after numerous ones attempted to correlate the material from three separate sets of transcripts, the vision dimmed, and it was not until Sue Malachuk waded through them and excitedly convinced me the message was preserved that "If It Please The King" was born.

My deepest gratitude to Sue, the Reed family, Shirlee, Karla and dear Wendy who re-typed it often enough to have it memorized.

To each of you, I say, thanks.

INTRODUCTION

We have heard much of "Arise, shine; for thy light is come, and the glory of the Lord is risen upon thee" (Isa. 60:1). We have heard it said that we have been created instruments of worship, and that it is the Lord's desire that we, the church, come into that obedience level where we can put the enemy to flight.

But the question that comes to us individually and certainly, corporately as the body of Christ is, How do we come from where we are living today to what we know He wants us to become? "I'm willing to do it, Lord. If there is any way You can do it in my lifetime, I'm willing for that. But, I don't know how to get from where I am now to that point. I don't know how to come out of my fears and my problems into that powerful position with You where I walk, live, move, talk, and have my being in You; where I have the mind of Christ; where the thoughts I think are not mine, they are Yours; where actions of my life are not mine, they are Yours. Lord I am willing but I don't know how."

I believe God will give us some absolutes as to how to get from this point to that point through the Book of Esther.

The Book of Esther is interesting because we know very little about the time it was written, who wrote it, or who the king was. He was probably Xerxes I, the son of Darius the Great. His Hebrew name of Ahasuerus corresponds directly with the Persian equivalent of Khshayarsha, usually known as Xerxes I, king of Persia from 486 to 465 B.C. and is the same Ahasuerus mentioned in Ezra 4:6. Then the feast of Esther 1:3, made by Ahasuerus in about 483 B.C., was to assemble the leading men of his empire to discuss a campaign against the Greeks to avenge the defeat of his father at Marathon in 490 B.C.

There is controversy about the Book of Esther. The name of God is not mentioned in the whole book and it was on that basis that it was almost dismissed from the Canon. Many questioned if this particular book was the inspired Word. Prayer is never mentioned; even so, we will devote one entire chapter to prayer.

Prior to 1980 the only message I had heard or preached from this book was taken from these words, "For such a time as this" (Esther 4:14). "Who knoweth whether thou art come to the kingdom for such a time as this?" We almost use that as slang. Every time someone says, "Why are you here?" or "What are you doing?", you say, "Well, it is for such a time as this." One day I became curious as to what preceded these words. And it was then that I became interested in this delightful book called "Esther."

While it is possible to over-type things from the Old Testament in our attempts to bring clarity, it is also possible to get "hung up" on types and shadows and numerical meanings such as: five is the number of grace; six is the number of man; and seven is the number of perfection. These have a place, however, when we begin to see that colors and numbers and symbols bring clarity to our understanding. You must also know that if you become extreme in these things, people may shy away from you. People can begin to fear you if you spend too much time on types and shadows and symbolism. Whenever we approach a book in the Bible, we need to find some keys to it.

There are key verses and key words which typify a synoptic study of Scripture. I presume the reader has had some teaching in this area. Also, we begin to find certain keys to personalities which unlock meanings.

I urge you to consider the characters and the meanings of their names as you study this book. As you progress, perhaps some of you will be teaching and ministering to others from Esther. Learn to look up all of these things. Remember that the Holy Spirit will bring the right key to your remembrance. But you can't remember something you have never learned. So, start learning. Learn the names. Look up the names of rivers and of people and of territories and of areas for your own understanding. Often it will give you the key to open a passage that has just been absolutely closed to you. Such was the case in my gaining an understanding of this book.

Let us look at some of the keys in the Book of Esther. Remember the keys that I give are not absolutes. I will show you certain people representing what I think are keys to this book. Someone else may come along and tell us that Esther does not represent the church, or, the "church within the church" as I'm going to say it. So don't get locked into what I give you. Be open enough to at least look at it and see if, in opening this book, we can't come to some clarity.

As we see early in the Book of Esther, the king appears to be a godless king. Because of this, few people would ever allow him to be a shadow or an example of Christ. But that's how we are going to see him, only in his role as king not by his life.

Esther differs from the other Jews. She is different from the other members of what would be called the nation of God. We speak of it, in New Testament terms, as the family of God. The way she is different is that she is totally controlled by Mordecai, who represents the Holy Spirit. Esther represents the bride of Christ, the church within the church.

Throughout this book, I use the phrase, the "church within the church." To bring clarification, I should say that I don't believe that every believer is in love with Jesus. I believe that all believers love Him. But, there is a vast difference between the two. And I believe that every believer is a member of the church, the *ecclesia,* 'the called out.' They have been born again. Resident within that church are those who are so in love with Jesus that they can never get enough. I refer to those as the church within the church. Immediately you say, "Well, I don't know which I am — whether I'm in love with Him or I just love Him." Usually those who are in the church within the church are a frustration to those who are not. They don't understand your hunger. They don't understand why you are not satisfied like they are.

The church without are those who have met Jesus as Saviour. They have almost a legal position with God. They know that Jesus died for their sins, that they were born in sin, shapen in iniquity, that they are doomed and bound for hell eternally if they don't know Jesus as Saviour. That is why we use the term "saved." Somewhere they heard a message which told them the truth that, if you don't repent of your sin and ask Him into your life, you are going to go to hell. That's that. So with a legalistic view to salvation from hell, they came to Him and said, "Lord, be merciful to me a sinner." The Lord said, "I hear that prayer." He saved them from sin, washed their sins away, cleansed them from unrighteousness and put Jesus Christ in them as the Saviour of their lives. They were totally satisfied with such a relationship.

There are others who said, "Well, this was good. Is there

more?" Someone replied, "Yes, there is a baptism in water, a circumcision of heart in representation. There is a baptism in the Holy Spirit." So they came even that far and received the baptism of the Holy Spirit, the gift of the Father. With the baptism of the Holy Spirit, many gifts were made manifest and they enjoyed the courting days.

You know what courting is all about, don't you? Men know how expensive it is and ladies know how much fun. Courting is that period of time when you get lots of gifts and you get to go out to eat often. Oh, we have had those experiences. When He just brought in teachers and preachers and He courted and courted. But there came a day, a very serious moment, when the Bridegroom looked at the church and said, "Will you marry me?"

Many people said, "No way. We don't want to get that involved." It is sadly true. "Now Lord, we love Your gifts and You are great. We really appreciate Your blessing, and we want You to bless us. That is wonderful, but You are asking for a commitment. That is kind of permanent. Besides, then I'll have to do dishes and take care of babies after I bring them forth." Many of them stepped back and said, "No, we like it like it is. Let's just have a good time." Others said, "Oh, yes, yes, I'll marry You! I've been waiting for this moment. To be in Your presence night and day, to know that we are one is the very cry of my spirit." Those are the church within the church.

I believe today that it is a new venture. It is a day when the Lord is saying to those of His bride, "No more games, no more flirtation, and not even courtship." We have been courted, and courted, and courted, many of us ever since we met Jesus and some of us since we were filled with the Holy Spirit. We have been given gifts; we have been taken out by the Lord to eat over and over, and this is the day of proposal. Do you accept? The Lord is saying, "Will you accept? Will you get this involved with Me? I am looking for a bride."

Now when this teaching came to the church, it was followed by the attitude or idea that because we were so special and so wonderful, we would be raptured first and everyone else would remain. I see something different. I see heightened responsibility coming to the bride which must be coupled with the prayer, "Thy kingdom come." We have heard bits and pieces and smatterings of revelation that have come through a variety of prophetic words that tell us that God plans to have the kingdom of God upon this earth. Yet, we have been totally careless about our attitude concerning it. Our attitude seems to have been one that says, "Do it, then. I mean, You are the Lord and if You are going to establish Your kingdom upon Your earth, great. We'll sit back and watch it and we'll rejoice in it." In order to get the job done, He has been searching. I believe that the searchlight of the Holy Spirit has been shining across the church for some time.

I believe that there were those of us whose hearts were so hungry after Him that without our knowledge, a choice was divinely made. We didn't know what we were volunteering for. The only thing we were saying was, "As the hart panteth after the water brooks, so panteth my soul after thee, O God" (Ps. 42:1).

Everything was wonderful. We felt so delighted in His presence and then suddenly it seemed that everything closed in on us. We entered a tunnel. The only light we saw was when we looked backwards. That is why in a lot of our churches we started doing the old things again, because they used to work. If the Lord didn't move, we moved anyway. If a chorus brought the presence of the Lord, we sang it twenty-four times. We did it in ignorance. We didn't know what else to do. Somehow we knew we had lost something. If we could be honest enough, we had the feeling we had lost our way. We didn't even have a new vision. We just knew one thing. We knew whom we had believed. We didn't have answers for each other. We didn't have answers for the world.

That wasn't difficult for the first year or two. We just said, "Praise the Lord. One day it is going to happen and we are going to know." We just kept walking, and then one day the cry came out of our spirits, Where are we going? What is the next move of God? We said, "Lord, we are tired of telling people we don't know. What are You going to do with us? If there isn't anything ahead, then help us to go back."

Come on, be honest. How many tried to go back? We picked up the old methods. We did everything we could to make things feel like they felt back there, and it didn't happen. So we said, "Let's find light." We looked backwards. It was too late. We had come too far into the tunnel. There we were, almost doomed.

What frustrated most of us was that the people who didn't enter the tunnel seemed happier than we were, and in the eyes of some, far more successful. They grew numerically; they grew financially; they looked like a total picture of success; and here we were groping and crying, "God, where are You?"

I believe that God has shown me that we are just about to come out of the other end of the tunnel. When we do there is going to be an unexpected revelation of God. Indeed in the next move of God many people are going to be praying for it all the way through it because they have designed in their thinking certain specific ways God will move, and He may not. But, He *will* move.

What has all this got to do with the bride? It is first to the bride, the church within the church, or the involved ones, that the next revelation will come. It is not circumstantial that traveling ministers lately have shared a cry of the Spirit encouraging people to get into a local church. It is not by chance that many others have heard that same voice saying, "Get yourself into a local church; submit yourself there; be known there; be a part of that body."

The next move of God is going to come through and to His church. Here is what is going to be frustrating about it. We would ordain then that there would be the church of the bride, or the church of the inner circle, or the church of the committed. I would ordain it that way, wouldn't you? How many would come if I would tell you where that church was? But within every local congregation there will be the church without and the church within. And to the people seated in those congregations who are totally involved with Him will come the greatest revelation and dimension of understanding they have ever known.

We are almost there. Don't you hear the wind blowing? There is something in the wind that is just stirring our hearts. God would caution us not to preconceive the how and what of it, rather to prepare our hearts to be recipients of and participants in it. We may miss it if we don't.

What He is calling for this day is total and complete involvement with Him to the separation of things in our lives that in themselves are not necessarily wrong. We are talking on a higher level. The path to holiness is often the elimination of things which are not sin of themselves. The things He lays His hand on we must release because He has something higher for us. What will we do when we get the revelation?

Do you remember that Jesus told the people, before the return of Christ there must come the return of Elijah? When John the Baptist came and he said, "Prepare ye the way of the

Lord, make his paths straight" (Matt. 3:3), the people listened and said, "Something is going to happen. We have to get ready." When Jesus came on the scene, He said, "Now that was Elijah," and the people were just a bit confused. What He was saying was, "There is a spirit of Elijah." Elijah was a forerunner. God has always had His prophets and His forerunners to speak ahead of time. I believe this will be the last time God will need a forerunner and He has no intention of it being one single ministry or one single denomination.

This time the spirit of Elijah is coming forth in the bride of Christ and she is going to say, "Oh, prepare ye the way of the Lord," as she stands in His presence, as she is illuminated in His light. As her very countenance radiates that light, she is going to say, "There is a great light among us."

God doesn't intend another charismatic outpouring. It is unnecessary. It is completed. The Lord doesn't have to repeat Himself. There is enough of His Holy Spirit in His church right now to break the power of hell in any city. We would rather pray that He does it than do our part in it.

But something is happening to the church within the church. I think the fact that we represent every place and background proves something. There is such a hungering, thirsting spirit in the bride of Christ that says, "Lord, I want to know You more." We are seeking the purposes of God. Now our purpose and our calling is about to be revealed to us through the Word, specifically, as we will see, through the Book of Esther. "For such a time as this" is the message of a forerunner. It is the message of an intercessor. We are going to see what God is going to ask from us in this next move when we emerge from this tunnel.

What is going to happen to the bride who is so in love with Him that she wants to be with Him? She is going to have the responsibility of coming out of the tunnel first, turning around, and shouting to those who aren't even sure they want to enter, "This is the way. Let me help you walk in it." They may say, "We don't need your help. We are richer and wiser and more sophisticated." We will reply, "Amen. But you are hungry and you are thirsty."

Some will come, some will not. Some of them will come all the way through the tunnel, groping as we did, stopping every now and then to shout to us, "Are you sure this is the way?" Our response must be, "It's the way! Just keep praising the Lord." Others may step in and step back out and step in.

What will we be doing? Everything in our natural sense would be saying, "That is what they deserve — we were the first." And the Bridegroom is going to say, "Ask them once more." The Lord says, "I'm married to the backslider." Wait a minute, were we talking about backsliders? Oh, yes, because any step back from progression is backsliding! Please hear it. They met Him as Saviour. That was enough that day, but the next day they should have been moving on. God doesn't intend there to be long spans of time between our maturity levels. Your highest experience in Him, He intended to be your lowest from that day on.

I

The King's Banquet

Esther 1

Now it came to pass in the days of Ahasuerus, (this is Ahasuerus which reigned from India even unto Ethiopia, over an hundred and seven and twenty provinces:)

That in those days, when the king Ahasuerus sat on the throne of his kingdom, which was in Shushan the palace,

In the third year of his reign, he made a feast unto all his princes and his servants; the power of Persia and Media, the nobles and princes of the provinces, being before him:

When he shewed the riches of his glorious kingdom and the honour of his excellent majesty many days, even an hundred and fourscore days. (1:1-4)

Let us discover the lessons of verses 1-4. It is a time when the king chooses, rather than the people choosing. The king chooses to invite all the people of power into his presence. He desires to reveal to them the riches of his glory. Isn't it interesting how we seem to think that we choose the time of revelation,

1

when clearly the Bible says, "Ye have not chosen me, but I have chosen you" (John 15:16)? When He invites you, behold, this is the day of your salvation; today is the accepted hour.

All through Scripture the indication is when He invites you, that is your time to respond. Every move of God, every revelation of God, every outpouring of God that you have studied in church history, every move of God that you have heard of from your ancestors, have come as a result of God being ready to reveal Himself. You say, "Wait a minute, it has always come as a result of someone praying and seeking the Lord." That is true. Let me ask you this. Why, all of a sudden, did a group of people get together and start to seek the Lord? Quite incredible isn't it that one day we have no appetite for Him, no desire and we are quite content; and the next day our souls thirst for God, and can't get enough of His Word?

That is what we have seen. The most recent move of God was the charismatic outpouring. It was a time when God was ready to reveal himself and pour out His Spirit upon all flesh. Well hath Jesus said, "Blessed are they which do hunger and thirst after righteousness: for they shall be filled" (Matt. 5:6). You cannot make yourself hungry; that comes from God. First comes the hunger, and second comes the invitation. The invitation always is contingent upon obedience. You have to wear certain garments. You have to come at certain times. How well we know that our time is not the Lord's. How many have tried to reprogram Him? So have I. How many know it doesn't work?

The invitation goes out to all the land and the king says, "I'm ready to show you my riches." If you really want to get excited about this, start looking up words that talk about revelation and riches. Go into the New Testament and read about the riches of His glory and see how those beautiful apostles have said, "He

2

has revealed unto us the riches of His grace and the riches of His glory."

> *And when these days were expired, the king made a feast unto all the people that were present in Shushan the palace, both unto the great and small, seven days in the court of the garden of the king's palace. (1:5)*

Seven is the number of fulfillment and perfection. It comes from a term that, if there were an apple tree with a green apple on it, I would say it was not perfect yet. The word really means ripe, fulfilled, ready to eat, ready to be partaken of. It may literally have been seven days; it may have only been a period of time, however long it took to fulfill the king's desire unto his people.

There is another sermon in the word 'garden.' Begin to look it up. It starts in the first book of the Bible, "And the Lord God took the man, and put him into the garden of Eden to dress it and to keep it" (Gen. 2:15). You will find a garden mentioned also in Isaiah and in Song of Solomon. We are told that we are the garden of the Lord. The same thing that was required of Adam in the first garden is required of us — being the garden. He was instructed to care for it and tend it. How do you care for a garden and tend it? Keep the weeds out, cultivate it, water it, and feed it.

> *Where were white, green, and blue, hangings, fastened with cords of fine linen and purple to silver rings and pillars of marble: the beds were of gold and silver, upon a pavement of red, and blue, and white and black, marble. (1:6)*

Everything here can have meaning. White speaks of purity;

3

green speaks of verdancy or of life and growth; blue speaks of the heavenlies. The fine linen speaks of the woven linen being part of the priests' garments. It speaks of Christ himself in perfection. Purple speaks of royalty, silver of refining. Marble in Scripture is that which is lasting, firm, polished, and beautiful to the sight. Gold is the most expensive metal spoken of in all of the Bible. What verse 6 is saying, is that the Lord is bringing everything precious and of value to His people.

They are gathered together. They have heard the call. The invitation has been issued to all. Many have come. The Bible does not say whether all who were invited came or not at this point. But, everyone who came saw the glory of the king. "But as many as received him, to them gave he power to become the sons of God, even to them that believe on his name" (John 1:12)

> And they gave them drink in vessels of gold, (the vessels being diverse one from another,) and royal wine in abundance, according to the state of the king. (1:7)

Here are all these people, and the servants are told to go out and give everyone a drink. It is not by chance that the next phrase is "(the vessels being diverse one from another,)." Don't overlook these things. Why is that there? Because so many of us want to be a vessel just like so-and-so. The Lord says, "You are my servant. I'm going to fill you with new wine. I want you to go out to my people and pour, pour, pour."

And we say, "Lord, if I could do it like so-and-so, I would." But if you could do it like so-and-so, He wouldn't need you. He's got so-and-so. So many times pastors say to me after a meeting, "We've enjoyed having you with us, but you are a bit frustrating

4

because you have said exactly what we have been saying all these months to our people. The only difference is that tonight they heard it."

I understand this because that precious pastor has been planting seeds out there, day after day, week after week. And the people are not hearing it. He's just the old common cup. So the Lord picks up the least likely of all of His children, and brings me to say the same thing another way. And it startles them, or as Scripture says, "provokes them" to hear and to listen. They say, "Oh, that makes all the sense in the world!"

It comes through me one way and him another, but it is the same wine. There is oil and wine in Zion. There are varieties of vessels and all have come through the purifying process. We are of different natures and personalities. Don't copy someone else. Just make sure you have the clear, pure wine.

". . . And royal wine in abundance, according to the state of the king." Notice that it did not say "barely enough to go around," but "wine in abundance." A friend and I were standing at the ocean some years back, as it is one of my favorite things to do. She said, "Do you know what I like about the ocean? It is something there is enough of." I thought, What a gorgeous description! That is the same description of the new wine, or the corn and wine from Zion, or the blessings and gifts of God. There are always enough to go around.

The only people who don't have enough to give are people who don't take enough in; people who don't know that the secret of prosperity is F-L-O-W. Anyone who takes unto themselves and keeps it is in trouble. We do that even with truths in Scripture. Suddenly we see something that we think no one has ever seen. It is a brand new revelation. It is so deep. We decide to save it for that right moment instead of allowing it to flow through us. The people that take unto themselves are poor. The only thing that they ever have is what they possess. People who give are constantly being refueled or refilled. The word is abundance. The kingdom principle is, Give and you shall receive.

"But my God shall supply all your needs according to his riches in glory by Christ Jesus" (Phil. 4:19), is another way of saying "according to the state of the king." "But, I don't want to ask Him for too much." Jesus said, "You have not because you ask not. Ask largely. Ask so that you may receive that your joy may be full."

> And the drinking was according to the law; none did compel: for so the king had appointed to all the officers of his house, that they should do according to every man's pleasure. (1:8)

I wish that were not a true precept and principle of God. I would prefer that it would be mandatory to drink. If it were up to me, I would force you all to the trough and hold your heads down until you had to drink. How many times have you tried to cram scripture down someone's throat? Or, you have tried to make them drink, or tried to make someone understand your revelation? And they said, "Listen, I don't see it," and you said, "Listen you *will* see it."

The godly principle of the very nature of Christ is to offer, not force. Offer, and that is what He is doing to you today. He is offering a drink of revelation of Himself. The law here shows us the New Testament principle, that He invites and that He is "not willing that any should perish, but that all should come to repentance" (2 Pet. 3:9). There are those who pick up that verse and say that means that ultimately everyone will be saved. Wrong. It means that ultimately everyone will be invited. It is what we do with what we have that makes the difference in our lives in the spiritual as well as the natural.

Here they are partaking together of what the king has given to them. I suppose one took one drink and said, "That is totally satisfying." There are thousands of Christians who will go to heaven, who have no desire or taste for more of God. They took one drink of wine and said, "That was tasty, delightful. Thank you so much." And we held the bottle saying, "There's more." "Oh, no, no more for me, I've got Jesus and that is enough." What will our attitude be toward these people? Superiority over them or rejection of them? Neither. The Bible says unto whom much is given, much is required. If we believe that we have taken a second drink, or a third, or more, it is then our responsibility to reach back and love them and bless them and receive them into the family of God. No one was penalized for drinking too much or too little.

> *Also Vashti the queen made a feast for the women in the royal house which belonged to king Ahasuerus. (1:9)*

Vashti is doing, as we would say, her thing. She is holding a meeting for the women, yet everything she does does not glorify the king. While everything she has and is has come from him, including the opportunity to hold the feast. Vashti has taken his power as her own and in so doing has lost the desire to please.

It is possible for churches and individuals to do the same thing. May we never hold a meeting that does not glorify our King. Everything we are belongs to Him. Everything we have has come from Him. How can I do less than give Him my best? He is everything. That is lordship as we understand it.

7

*On the seventh day, [There is the number again
meaning completion. On the day of this completion, in other words, everything that has preceded
this has been fulfilled.] when the heart of the king
was merry with wine, he commanded Mehuman,
Biztha, Harbona, Bigtha, and Abagtha, Zethar, and
Carcas, the seven chamberlains that served in the
presence of Ahasuerus the king, (1:10)*

He brought in his servants. That's what that verse means. If
you want to dig it out you can read some different descriptions
and meanings of their names. And the purpose was:

*To bring Vashti the queen before the king with
the crown royal, to shew the people and the princes her beauty: for she was fair to look on. (1:11)*

In certain circles, some people maintain that this is a man
who is using his wife just to show her off. We dare not see this as
the desire of a king to exploit his wife while in the state of
drunkenness. Rather let us see it as the king giving opportunity
to his bride to reveal the beauty that is a result of her having been
prepared for him.

Some of the names in this passage have interesting meanings. King Ahasuerus means two things. It means "I will be
silent" and "I will be poor." If we are thinking of our King Jesus,
what Scripture might that remind you of prophetically? "As a
sheep before her shearers is dumb, so he openeth not his
mouth" (Isa. 53:7). He was silent. He divested himself of all
earthly things. Remember when John's disciples said, "Where
do you live?" And Jesus said, "The Son of man hath not where

to lay his head" (Luke 9:58). Jesus never made excuses for the glory that was in Him or the glorious things He did, for He knew that His mission was to reveal the Father. With that same purpose and boldness, our commission is to reveal Him also. That is why we are told to "Let your light so shine before men, that they may see your good works, and glorify your Father which is in heaven" (Matt. 5:16).

The king's desire is to bring Vashti into the spotlight. Vashti's name means "why" or "where doth thou go banqueting?" Why then, when the king is so merry, does he send for Vashti? And whom might she represent? Yes, she is the church which has that universal call to be those in whom the world beholds the beauty of the king. Everything beautiful about us; anything we have that is of value; His anointing, His blessing, have come from Him. We will see that clearly as we proceed through this beautiful book.

He knows what He has put within you. And there are days in your life when He calls you and the purpose is that He might reveal His beauty in you and through you. He may remove you from one situation and place you in another, so that His beauty and His glory may be seen. He literally wants to parade you in front of people to whet their appetites. And we sit back and say, "Oh, no," feeling very humble and being very disobedient.

> *But the queen Vashti refused to come at the king's commandment by his chamberlains: therefore was the king very wroth, and his anger burned in him. (1:12)*

Why is the "but" there? The "but" is related to the previous statement. She was invited and she had been beautified. She had everything that was necessary to fulfill the invitation but she refused.

That is what we do every time we hear a sermon, that we don't appropriate to our living levels.

"Therefore was the king very wroth, and his anger burned in him." What verse does this remind you of? "My spirit shall not always strive with man" (Gen. 6:3). As we go through this book and you get an understanding of a scripture, such as this, ask yourself if there are any other verses that would support this revelation. You know that the only true interpretation of Scripture is Scripture itself. Because Scripture supports these thoughts, I am permitted to utilize them, and there are many such supporting verses.

> *Then the king said to the wise men, which knew the times, (for so was the king's manner toward all that knew law and judgment: (1:13)*

There were the children of Issachar and it was said of them that they "had understanding of the times" (I Chron. 12:32). God desires always to have such a people. Of such were the sons of Zadok. In Ezekiel 44:23 we are told that the priests unto the Lord "shall teach my people the difference between the holy and profane." In the New Testament, we read these words from I John 2:27, 20: "Ye need not that any man teach you. But ye have an unction [or an anointing] from the Holy One."

We are His church. Jesus Christ is the foundation and God knows every living stone which has been builded together to constitute His temple. It is in this temple that His Spirit dwells. This spirit described in Isaiah 11:2,3 is the enablement for godly counsel and proper judgment when called for by the King.

10

> *And the next unto him was Carshena, Shethar,*
> *Admatha, Tarshish, Meres, Marsena, and Memu-*
> *can, the seven princes of Persia and Media, which*
> *saw the king's face, and which sat the first in the*
> *kingdom;) (1:14)*

Those who have His wisdom are those who know Him. Those who know Him are those who come consistently before His face. "If my people, which are called by my name, shall humble themselves, and pray, and seek my face" (2 Chron. 7:14). Often we don't seek His face. We do pray, well, at least we offer Him a "want list." What does it mean to seek the face of the Lord? Perhaps the best way to say it would be, "That I may know him, and the power of his resurrection, and the fellowship of his sufferings" (Phil. 3:10). Our cry then has to be, "Oh, I want to be before Your face. I want to know God." He says, "To those of you who know Me, who come before My face, who kow My ways, I can entrust My wisdom."

". . . And which sat the first in the kingdom." God is no respecter of persons, but spiritual authority is delegated to those who truly know their God. The beauty of the promise, "Seek and ye shall find," eliminates any feelings that God has favorites. Those who only seek His power may be seekers of positional authority rather than seekers of God, and therefore unqualified for divine promotion.

> *What shall we do unto the queen Vashti accord-*
> *ing to law, because she hath not performed the*
> *commandment of the king Ahasuerus by the*
> *chamberlains? (1:15)*

The king is saying that the law has been broken and the

11

question is, What shall be the result? "The wages of sin is death" (Rom. 6:23). To persist in sin merits eternal death, but there are other deaths that come to us by the sin of not obeying the King such as the deaths of opportunity, revelation, and growth.

Sadly, Vashti never answered the question, "Where, or why doth thou go banqueting?" Checking our motives is a daily responsibility. "Let the words of my mouth, and the meditation of my heart, be acceptable in thy sight, O Lord, my strength and my redeemer" (Ps. 19:14) should be our daily prayer. Vashti ignored this and as a result refused an opportunity to come before the face of the king. She was content to just act in his name. Where do we do our feasting and why? Where are we spending our time, our energies, and our efforts? She has turned the king down and he has spoken to those whom he has called and asked what they think ought to be done.

> And Memucan answered before the king and the princes, Vashti the queen hath not done wrong to the king only, but also to all the princes, and to all the people that are in all the provinces of the king Ahasuerus.
>
> For this deed of the queen shall come abroad unto all women, so that they shall despise their husbands in their eyes, when it shall be reported, The king Ahasuerus commanded Vashti the queen to be brought in before him, but she came not.
>
> Likewise shall the ladies of Persia and Media say this day unto all the king's princes, which have heard of the deed of the queen. Thus shall there arise too much contempt and wrath.
>
> If it please the king, let there go a royal com-

mandment from him, and let it be written among the laws of the Persians and the Medes, that it be not altered, That Vashti come no more before king Ahasuerus; and let the king give her royal estate unto another that is better than she.

And when the king's decree which he shall make shall be published throughout all his empire, (for it is great,) all the wives shall give to their husbands honour, both to great and small.

And the saying pleased the king and the princes; and the king did according to the word of Memucan:

For he sent letters into all the king's provinces, into every province according to the writing thereof, and to every people after their language, that every man should bear rule in his own house, and that it should be published according to the language of every people. (1:16-22)

Let us see here that it is impossible to sin and only involve yourself. Your sinning and your disobedience have an effect on others, whether it be a neighbor or someone with whom you work or your children or friends. It is a far-reaching thing.

Foolish is the person who believes that he can disobey the King and not affect others. Isn't that incredible? So the decree has gone out. If Vashti does not want to come before the face of the king, the king shall not do without. God will have a people in whom He will reveal Himself. It is here we see a picture of the Jews or the nation of Israel as they are given first opportunity to become God's people.

You might want to study Ezekiel 16 with this. When God

through Ezekiel speaks, He says, "Ezekiel, tell my people Israel that I found them when they were like a dying child out in a field. They were nothing. I didn't choose them because they were mighty and great and beautiful. I chose them because they were the least likely to succeed, and I knew that if any good came out of them, I would get the glory." He said, "You were nothing." And He said, "I chose you." Why? Why did God choose Israel? What was the reason if He is no respecter of persons?

The whole purpose in God choosing Israel was that Israel was going to have the glory of God put upon them so that they would be powerful and wealthy. And then they were to go to every nation on earth and reveal the source of their power and the source of their wealth. They were to be the revelation of Jehovah God to the earth. Instead they took the glory to themselves. They caused fear in everyone else. They went whoring, as Ezekiel 16 and some of the prophets declare. They walked away from God in their own pride.

That is where we see Vashti. Everything she has is given her by the king, but he is not truly her lord. While it is true that God will find those who walk in obedience and come before His presence at His command, it is equally true that those who refuse are excluded from that intimacy of communion and increase of power which was to have been their royal estate. The question is obvious, isn't it? Is He your Lord? Is He your God? How do you know if He is Lord? Does he consume the majority of your thought time? Not simply did you do what He last ordered you to do? That would make Him your commander in chief. But do you think upon His principles? How you may please Him? "Lord, am I pleasing You in my job? Am I pleasing You in my study? Am I pleasing You in my social life? Am I pleasing You?"

If that is the majority of your thinking then you can probably relax with the knowledge that Jesus Christ is indeed Lord of your life. If your attitude is, "I'll go when I'm in the mood; I'll do what I want to do, when I want to do it," then it may be that you are facing a day when the Lord will say, "Oh, how I would have . . . ." Does that remind you of any verse? Jesus said, "Jerusalem, Jerusalem, . . . how often would I have gathered thy children together, even as a hen gathereth her chickens under her wings, and ye would not!" (Matt. 23:37). Oh, what we could have in the Lord, and how we refuse it.

O King Eternal, thank You for Your gracious invitation to enjoy the food You so bountifully have prepared for me. Teach me to never be so busy doing things in Your name that I miss the opportunity of Your presence. Help me to walk in obedience and submission to You at all times proving the only motivation of my life to be that I may please the king. Amen.

II

A Prepared Bride

Esther 2:1-14

Chapter two introduces a whole new subject, a new thought. We are about to see someone else enter the scene.

> *After these things, when the wrath of king Aha-*
> *suerus was appeased, he remembered Vashti, and*
> *what she had done, and what was decreed*
> *against her. (2:1)*

This is very consistent with God's wrath being appeased. When judgment has been met, God's wrath is always appeased. In the Old Testament, God had to allow the Chaldeans and the Assyrians to come in and take His people captive at different times. Then His wrath against His own people was appeased.

In the New Testament what is that? The cross, Calvary. When Jesus took upon himself our sin, He literally became sin and He became the perfect lamb spoken of in Exodus 12. He fulfilled it all, and God's wrath was appeased. That is why we pray through the name of Jesus. It is through Christ we come to God.

We have no right to come to God except through Christ. We deserve judgment, the punishment of death. We deserve for

17

Him to say, "You may never come before my face," because there are times in our lives when we have not come. But when we come through Jesus, He says, "My wrath is appeased through Christ." No wonder we sing so much about that name above all names, the name of Jesus.

"He remembered Vashti, and what she had done, and what was decreed against her." This verse is a picture of the mercy and the never failing love of our Saviour. He looks on the Jews today. His heart grieves for them; He longs for them; He still wants them to receive Him. There will be a time when revelation will be made clear to them; and as many as will receive Christ will claim their inheritance. It is not because they are special of themselves. They are special because He loves them. God so loved, that He gave . . . They are His people, and His cry to them is as it was when Jesus was upon the earth. The king's servants see this cry and they see the desire of the king. They know he is thinking, Oh, I wish she had come. I wanted Vashti to come that I might reveal her.

> Then said the king's servants that ministered unto him, Let there be fair young virgins sought for the king:
>
> And let the king appoint officers in all the provinces of his kingdom, that they may gather together all the fair young virgins unto Shushan the palace, to the house of the women, unto the custody of Hege the king's chamberlain, keeper of the women; and let their things for purification be given them:
>
> And let the maiden which pleaseth the king be queen instead of Vashti. And the thing pleased the king; and he did so. (2:2-4)

18

The story in Matthew 22 is of the king who prepared a wedding for his son. He invited the guests but they had excuses for not attending. Despite their refusal, the king would have wedding guests. A commandment was issued to his servants to seek out any who would respond to his invitation and attend wearing the wedding garment. The people came, the place was filled, and the merriment began. Suddenly, one was spotted without the wedding garment. The Bible says that person had to be put out. The lesson for us in this story is that every invitation from the King for increased fellowship demands not merely the desire to accept, it demands preparation.

We begin to identify with Esther as the Gentiles. We have been grafted in, the Scripture says. Where the nation Israel refused the invitation, the Lord said, "I will reach out to the Gentiles and give them the opportunity to reveal my glory to the world. I will trust them to be faithful to show the riches that I put upon them and give Me the glory and credit."

Why would God want the credit? Is God some kind of ego-maniac sitting upon a throne saying, "I will give this to you; then you go out and brag on Me"? We don't like to admit it, but I think sometimes we have that concept. No, my friend, the reason He wants everyone to acknowledge Him, the source of glory, is because if they come to that source, they too will receive. If they only see it as you — Oh, what a wonderful ministry you have; Oh, what a wonderful this you have — they will never receive it. They will only sit back and worship you or envy you at the highest. But he says, "Oh, if they know that I am your source, then they will know that they too can have that." That is why God wanted Israel to reveal Him to every nation; that the whole world might be saved.

> *Now in Shushan the palace there was a certain Jew, whose name was Mordecai, the son of Jair, the son of Shimei, the son of Kish, a Benjamite;*
> *Who had been carried away from Jerusalem with the captivity which had been carried away with Jeconiah king of Judah, whom Nebuchad-nezzar the king of Babylon had carried away.*
> *And he brought up Hadassah, that is Esther, his uncle's daughter: for she had neither father nor mother, and the maid was fair and beautiful; whom Mordecai, when her father and mother were dead, took for his own daughter. (2:5-7)*

"Now in Shushan the palace there was a certain Jew." I'm not trying to play on words, but I'm trying to show you how to dig things out of Scripture. That is one of my desires. Walk yourself through some verses and learn what it means when it says "certain." On a certain day, at a certain place, at a certain time, an angel came to a certain woman and said a certain thing. You will begin to discover the beauty of the individual treatment from God. Aren't you glad that we are not just all amassed into being Gentiles or Jews? Aren't you glad that on a certain day, a certain God sent a certain person to you to say a certain thing that triggered a certain response? Hallelujah! And certainly we have been called.

The Hebrew word for Esther is Hadassah. Hadassah means, the myrtle. Esther has two meanings. It means, I will be hidden. It also means, a star. That will have far more clarity when we finish chapter two.

As Mordecai enters the picture, we see the work of the Holy Spirit in the life of the believer preparing us for the king. Mordecai means, one who is concerned. The name also means oppressed or bitterness. The Holy Spirit, Mordecai, is often grieved or bitter or hurt when we do not obey or are unprepared to stand before the King. It is, of course, the work of the Holy Spirit to take the invitation of the King, bring it to us, have us accept, and then prepare us to be the bride of Christ. Do we acquiesce to that? That is what is going on inside of you right now. That is why we are destined for change. Beholding Him, we are changed. That will be the fulfillment of pleasing the King.

Our time here on earth is our opportunity to enter the college of the chosen. Our new birth enrolls us and each has an assigned time period before graduation. In the last days the trumpets shall sound, the angels shall say, "Time shall be no more." So that period of time that is from birth to death, is simply allotted to us while He is getting us ready to be His bride. God help us to redeem the time.

> *So it came to pass, when the king's command-*
> *ment and his decree was heard, and when many*
> *maidens were gathered together unto Shushan*
> *the palace, to the custody of Hegai, that Esther was*
> *brought also unto the king's house, to the custody*
> *of Hegai, keeper of the women. (2:8)*

During this time when many are answering this call, coming into the palace, and being put in the custody Hegai, Mordecai brings Esther. What is the first thing she has to learn? Submission to authority. Submission to authority is a lesson of life. That is why the Bible talks about husbands and wives and mutual submission one to another. Marriage is probably the easiest place to learn the lesson of submission, but many of us did not

21

learn it within the realms of marriage. That doesn't eliminate the course.

How many times have we taken the course over on some things? We will learn to submit to authority. We will learn it because it is an eternal lesson. God is a God or order. There is placement of authority. We don't mind submitting to people when we really trust them. If we vote them in, we can submit. because, somehow, we feel we are still in charge. If I am in support of one who is in charge, I can support him and bless him and encourage him. If he should trip, I say, "Listen, that's all right. Get right back up." But, if one is in a position over me whom I do not support, I just wait for him to fall. We will learn the lesson if we are ever to become His bride.

God is going to allow the enemy's searchlight to shine on the church. We are being given an opportunity now to clean up our lives. But soon, I believe, God is going to say to the world, "All right, look them over. You have been wanting a good look at them. Shine your light on my church. See if they are not all in submission to Me, rightly related in their homes, in their churches, and in their families. See if they haven't learned the lesson of submission."

The day you said, "Jesus, be Lord of all the kingdoms of my life," you said, "Holy Spirit, wholly possess me, make me completely yours. Lead me to Him. Allow me to know Him in fullness." Whatever your words were, what you did was give Him license to rule your life. Now He waits for that right moment. You are already submitted, but you are not commissioned. We dread that interim period between submitting and being commissioned.

When the Holy Spirit uproots us from one setting to another, our fear and insecurity questions, "Holy Spirit, whose custody are You going to put us in?" He is going to put us into the custody of Hegai, meaning my meditations. We are going to learn to meditate on the Word. Up until now, many of us have been spoon-fed. We take a sermon, mix it, and add milk. You know what I mean. Our mouths are pried open, and the food is crammed down, and we go away full.

There comes a time when the Holy Spirit steps in and says, "Feed yourself!" It is frustrating to people when that happens because I'll tell you how it comes. Everything you hear ministered across the pulpit, you have already heard. And that is so frustrating. You are waiting for new truth. "Give me something new. I know that. I mean it is good for those who don't know the Lord, but I need to hear something new." That is God's way of saying to you, Get yourself into the Word and learn to eat it. You need to spend some time in it. "Thy word have I hid in mine heart, that I might not sin against thee" (Ps. 119:11).

You need to know the Word. It is your life source. It is everything that you are going to be judged by. It isn't good enough just to hear me talk about it. It isn't good enough just to hear your pastor. Learn to get into it yourself. It doesn't matter how long it takes. We don't even know. Esther is brought into Hegai.

And the maiden pleased him, and she obtained kindness of him; and he speedily gave her her things for purification, with such things as belonged to her, and seven maidens which were meet [equipped] to be given her, out of the king's house: and he preferred her and her maids unto the best place of the house of the women. (2:9)

How can the Word do that for us? By heeding it. God's Word is _for_ you. It is not against you. His Word is to bless your life. His Word is the key to success in business. The principles to be found in the Word are the keys to successful marriages. His Word is the key to successful living.

He gave her what belonged to her. You have some talents and some abilities innately. You developed some culturally and environmentally as you grew up in your homes and so on. There are some things you can do. And it is most ridiculous when I see Christians, who are very capable in certain areas, but feel it is less than spiritual to develop their talents. They try to involve themselves in something they are not capable of so that they can wholly lean on the Lord, failing to recognize Him as creator and giver. His Word is our guide for implementing the gifts in such a way as to bring glory to Him.

He will also begin to add to you. We grow from glory to glory, from grace to grace. "The path of the just is as the shining light, that shineth more and more unto the perfect day" (Prov. 4:18). Everything is progressive in Scripture for the believer. He is not going to lock you into what you are today. He is going to change you and add to you and utilize some things that you have. And when you take the talent He has given you and invest it instead of hiding it, He comes back to double it or multiply it ten times over. That is the principle of the New Testament.

"And he preferred her and her maids unto the best place." The Lord wants to promote you. "Promotion cometh neither from the east, nor from the west, nor from the south" (Ps. 75:6). Promotion cometh from the Lord. Perhaps some of you have never been delivered from being people-pleasers. You think that if you treat so-and-so just right and say the things that they want to hear, since they have the power, they will promote you. If they promote you, and you take your orders from them, I promise

24

you that you will also take your rewards from them. We need to begin to understand what it means to say, "Lord, I belong to You. Whatosever You say unto me, I will do."

> *Esther had not shewed her people nor her kindred: for Mordecai had charged her that she should not shew it. (2:10)*

Esther was a Jew. She would not have been allowed in the king's palace if this fact had been known. Is there ever a time when the Holy Spirit reveals something to you and then says, "Don't share it right now"? The answer to that question is yes. There will be times when something will be revealed to you and the Holy Spirit will say to you, "Hold it for yourself. I will tell you when to speak and when to be silent. I will tell you when to reveal and when not to reveal."

The law of the priesthood is that you will always receive more than you ever give. The instruction to the priest was to receive the offering, place it in a boiling pot, and the first piece of meat from the pot was to be eaten by him (1 Sam. 2:13-15). The remainder was to be shared with the others. Unless we understand this as a principle, we can become frustrated at receiving more than we are capable of giving.

Paul said, "For I have received of the Lord that which also I delivered unto you (1 Cor. 11:23). You should always get more than you give. That is the law of the priesthood. How sad it is to sometimes see that law in reverse.

> *Now when every maid's turn was come to go in to king Ahasuerus, after that she had been twelve months, according to the manner of the women,*

(for so were the days of their purifications accom-
plished, to wit, six months with oil of myrrh, and
six months with sweet odours, and with other
things for the purifying of the women.) (2:12)

Here she is. Esther has been brought into the Word, and
called to study to show herself approved unto God. She is
learning to meditate on the Word and to feed herself. She is
there for a period of time. But have you noticed some other
things are taking place? For six months some things are happening here. She is being bathed with oil of myrrh.

The ingredients for the anointing oil are spoken of individually in Exodus 30. There were certain ingredients and certain
amounts. Myrrh indeed was one (Exod. 30:23). In fact, five
hundred shekels of myrrh were part of these spices that were to
be added to the olive oil. They had to be mashed to be fragrant.
Myrrh is a plant that is very bitter to taste, but extremely fragrant
to smell. We will all experience that in our lives. The bitter things
that we have to endure. How painful those moments can be.
They smell sweet, but they are bitter. Your feelings are, God, why
do I have to go through this? There can be no glory in this. But
each one of us looking back through our lives can point to that
spice, take a big breath, and say, "Oh, what it has taught me."
How good it smells. And if you have properly learned your
lesson, it also benefits those around you because they sense the
fragrance of what that hard lesson has taught you.

The second spice was sweet cinnamon, two hundred fifty
shekels of it. Sweet cinnamon is just the opposite of myrrh. It
has a very disagreeable odor, but anything you put cinnamon in
tastes better. In other words, it improves the taste of anything
bitter. This speaks to me of the joys and blessings of life which
help us endure the bitter.

But to be very practical, this also speaks to me of channels or vessels who are not pretty or handsome. Maybe we don't like the way they speak. Maybe the level of their voice is not what we would enjoy. It's too low, it's too high, it's too raspy, it's too something. We just don't like them. They don't dress like we want them to. They don't wear the fragrances we like. Everything external about them "turns us off." Yet God may use this very vessel to pour forth the water for which we thirst and the taste of that is sweet.

Calamus, two hundred fifty shekels of calamus. This is an interesting plant, because it scents the air while it is growing. The tiniest plant has a fragrance and the taller it grows, the greater will be the fragrance. At every level of your maturity, there is something fragrant that can come forth from your life, if you allow it. When you are an infant in the Lord, at least you can talk about Jesus as Saviour. And when you are first baptized you can talk about that. There should always be a fragrance coming forth from your life.

Cassia, five hundred shekels. This plant only grows at very high elevations and has purple flowers. Purple speaks of dignity, of course, of Christ's royal nature. It also tells you about those times you have mountain-peak experiences. It is glorious to be there. It also says you are the King's kid and you need to get your head out of the sand, and begin to walk and live like a King's kid. Begin to know who you are.

Charisma is a word that means unction or smearing on. We derive our word anointing from it. In other words, just as Esther, every one of us must allow the Holy Spirit to lead us into situations that seem unpleasant sometimes to taste, sometimes to smell, sometimes small such as the little plant, sometimes glorious as the large plant. We must allow Him to lead us into those situations so that each spice may be smeared upon us as a lesson that becomes a blessing of life.

There are other names for these spices and various descriptions given them, all of which can typify increased spiritual understanding.

Now, Esther has been anointed for a period of time. Six months with one thing and she just gets out of that, then six months with another. In chapter 2 verse 9 we are told that seven maidens are going to administer the ointment for her purification. Often the very people who bring the myrrh, and the cinnamon, and the cassia and the calamus to us are the people we want to dismiss from our lives, not realizing that they are the tools God uses for our purification. That is what Jesus meant when He said, "Bless your enemies. You need them. Without them you don't grow."

And Mordecai walked every day before the court of the women's house, to know how Esther did, and what should become of her. (2:11)

How grateful are we that He never just appoints us to a place and leaves us? Every day the Holy Spirit is back in your life saying, "How are you doing today? Do you understand the Word? Do you know what you are reading? Are you meditating on it?" How we learn to appreciate the promptings of the Holy Spirit.

When Saul was on the road to Damascus, Jesus said to him, "It's hard for you to kick against the pricks." What were the pricks? The first prick probably came when Stephen died. Saul saw that great light and that beautiful man saying, "Lord, lay not this sin to their charge" (Acts 7:60). Despite this demonstration of love and forgiveness, and the glory of God, Saul determined to deny it.

It is hard for you to kick against the pricks, too. Mordecai is there every day of your life revealing and comforting. You may feel alone, but you are not alone. He knows exactly where you are, and He never asks from you any more than you are capable of giving.

Every maiden's turn was come, and the purifications were accomplished. And when it was time (v. 13) for them to go into the king, each maiden would be given whatever she desired to take with her to the king's house. There is a maturity level in your life where the Lord says to you, "What do you want?" He can't do that to a four year old. You ask the four year old what they want for Christmas, and even though they live on the twenty-eighth floor of an apartment house, they could very likely ask for a pony. "We could keep him in the flower box." You know; they don't.

Some of us have similar approaches to the Lord. "Lord, grant me power and authority." And if He did, we would kill everyone on the road who drove ten miles an hour slower than we did. But there does come a time in our maturity when the Holy Spirit says to us, "What would you like that you don't have? What would you want Me to put upon you so that you could come before my presence?"

In the evening she went in (v. 14). On the morrow she returned to the second house of the women. Now she goes to a different place. You see, the work has been done. That doesn't mean we ever leave the Word. It means that the Word is so within us that we go on and are able to be builded with the Word within us.

She has gone through the whole preparation and purification

time. It is time for her to be brought before the king to see if he accepts her. If he does not, she waits to see if ever he will, and she returns to Shaashgaz. This name literally means, who succoured the cutoff. To give you an understanding of it, it means the weaner; the one who does the weaning. She has been with Hegai, meditator. She has been meditating in the Word. She has come through the purification, all the problems of her life. The Holy Spirit, Mordecai, is constantly by her side. Now she is to be brought before the king, and she has to come the next day into the custody of Shaashgaz. She needs to be weaned from the things of the past to get on with the things of the future.

Some people only talk about the six months of myrrh. Other people talk about the six months of oil. "I will never forget when I was so filled with the Holy Spirit. I did this, and I did that, and I went there." Or, "I'll never forget when I was going through . . . ." And the Lord is saying to the church, "Grow up," and that demands not living in the past.

I think we are going to come into a literal fulfillment of Isaiah 60, if this generation will adhere to what the Spirit is saying today. But there has to be something that happens to us between the experience of the past and the revelation of the future.

That seems to be where the church is today. We are between Hegai, the meditation and that move of God, the dealings of God, and the next great revelation, which, I believe, will bring us before the presence of the King of Kings and the Lord of Lords. And in between, there has to be a Shaashgaz. There has to be something that succours; that nurtures that cutoff; that teaches us how to walk a new life. Everything about this chapter relates to learning to live a new life.

For too many years, the church has been less than beautiful to anyone but the church. But when His beauty is set upon us, I believe the world is going to begin to look at the church to find out, "How come some things work for you that don't work for us?" I believe the beauty of Christ is going to be revealed in His church. The words of an old chorus of my church background are:

> *Let the beauty of Jesus be seen in me;*
> *All His wonderful passion and purity.*
> *Oh, thou Spirit divine; all my nature refine;*
> *Until the beauty of Jesus is seen in me.*

Father, let this be my cry this day. I pray that You would set Your beauty upon me as You will, and then use it to the praise of Your glory. Amen.

III

An Accepted Bride

Esther 2:15-20

Now Esther has been brought in, in prophetic fulfillment. "Instead of the brier shall come up the myrtle tree" (Isa. 55:13). As previously stated, Hadassah, Esther's name, means myrtle. Esther, the Jewish term for Hadassah, means hidden and a star. We are about to see her come forth from her hidden position for she has undergone some things, among them six months of preparation. How many have been able to identify with Esther in that?

You understand that we are saying there are seasons. There are periods of time in our lives when it seems like everything is going against us. If we can see that on a higher level in what we speak of as faith, that is a blessing. The maidens were given to her to administer the ointment. This time is especially wonderful when you pass through it because it has perfected something. Psalm 138:8 says, "The Lord will perfect that which concerneth me." To some people that is a promise and to others it may be a threat.

Then there followed six months of sweet spices. You also have periods of your life where you are so successful. Everything you do is anointed. Every prayer you pray gets answered.

33

There are wonderful times when you just feel spiritual, and know that you are where God wants you. Nothing can shake you; winds blow, people try to dissuade you, and you say, "I know that I know that I know." They are wonderful seasons but yet untested. Psalm 4:1 says, "Thou hast enlarged me when I was in distress."

Now Esther has come, and she has spent these two periods of time. She has learned to medidate in the Word. She has then been passed on to Shaashgaz, who will succour the cutoff, which is what his name means. In other words, he is weaning her from the past. I trust that the Holy Spirit will teach you that it is not overnight that we forget the things of the past.

In Joshua 1, the Lord said to Joshua, "Moses my servant is dead." Now that can't have been a shock. Joshua has just come out of thirty days of mourning. He knows Moses is dead. Why did the Lord feel it necessary to say, "Joshua, Moses is dead?" Joshua's answer would have to be, "I know that." And yet do we? Some of us are still nursing our Moses, the good old past. "I'll never forget when brother so-and-so . . . ." You know what I'm saying. And so Shaashgaz comes to help us sever the past.

> Now when the turn of Esther, the daughter of Abihail the uncle of Mordecai, who had taken her for his daughter, was come to go in unto the king, she required nothing but what Hegai the king's chamberlain, the keeper of the women, appointed. And Esther obtained favour in the sight of all them that looked upon her. (2:15)

It is time for Esther to come before the presence of the king, to see if he likes what he sees. She is given this opportunity, "You may add anything you like to what has already been done." Seemingly, all the other maidens have added whatever was important to them: wealth, talent, silk gowns, jewelry, furs, and so on. Perhaps we would think of it spiritually as, "If I could have this ministry, or if I could be in that situation, I would please the Lord." Esther comes to this point and she says, "I want only whatever you think I ought to have" (v. 15). As a result of this, Esther obtained favor in the sight of all those who looked upon her.

Truly the Word is our mirror. When the beauty that He has put upon us is all on which we depend, it will so enhance our whole being that others will see Christ and glorify Him, because they see Him in us. Jesus said, "If the world hated Me, it will hate you." We haven't understood that Jesus, in that instance, wasn't talking about individuals at all; He was talking about the world system. And so we feel very pure when the world rejects us because of our spirituality. The fact is that they ought to like us more because there is more and more of Jesus.

> So Esther was taken unto king Ahasuerus into
> his house royal in the tenth month, which is the
> month Tebeth, in the seventh year of his reign.
> (2:16)

At last, an entrance into his presence, and the king loved Esther above all the women. She obtained favor. There is a tremendous key in the word "obtained," because we have a tendency to read it "attained." One is grace, the other is what we earn. She obtained, because she was prepared by the king's servants and added nothing of herself. She had no earthly right to be there, yet the Holy Spirit had led her.

Who are you? Who am I? that I dare to enter and stand boldly before the throne of grace and mercy and say to Him, "I adore You. I worship You." Why am I not ignored or dismissed? Because the Holy Spirit one day spoke to my heart and led me through the blood, through the flesh of the Lord Jesus Christ. And it is in Christ that I stand boldly before His throne.

Many times we have felt the way Esther felt, and maybe even as those women who were not chosen to go in before the king, for as you heard in our story, this is the coming before the king after all of the preparation. I wonder if we don't sometimes think that the reason we are permitted to come before the king is because of some consecration we have recently made. Isn't that subtle? We perhaps word it a little better, but I think what we really say to the Lord, when we want to come before Him is, "Lord, I've been good; I haven't done the things You told me not to do, and I have indeed done the things You told me to do, and so, Lord, I come into Your presence." How many of you know you never get there?

A songwriter some time ago said, "I've sacrificed a lot of things to walk this narrow way. I gave up fame and fortune and I'm worth a lot to Thee. And then I heard Him gently say to me, 'I left a throne of glory and counted it but loss; my feet were nailed in anguish upon a cruel cross.'" You see, the Bible says, "Herein is love, not that we loved God, but that he loved us" (1 John 4:10). It can be frustrating for us to realize that we can't even love Him unless He gives us the love to give back to Him. We cannot praise Him unless He puts the praise within our hearts to do so. We can only bless the King with what He has already given to us.

And so Esther obtained grace. Grace so often is defined as unmerited favor, and indeed it means that. But it has a much stronger meaning than, "Well, I didn't deserve it but I got it."

Among other things, grace means to stoop to a person of lesser degree to perform an act of kindness. We can never rise to a level where we earn His grace. We can never find that "I'll live for Him who died for me" on a reciprocal basis. Everything we are for the rest of our lives cannot repay the love debt we owe.

Esther comes before his presence on this first visit. She doesn't know what is going to happen. Perhaps that is the most frustrating part of Him being in control. We still have those little tendencies to want to know steps one, two, three, and four. If I yield myself totally to Him, what will He ask for? What will He do? We need to recognize that fear is a preventative to coming into the presence of the Lord.

Recall with me the story in Exodus 19. The Lord had been visiting with Moses in a very beautiful way; in such a way that His presence was like a cloud on top of the mountain. Moses would go up on the mountain to be with the Lord. One time the Lord said, "Moses, I'd like to visit with all of the congregation. Gather them about the mountain; have them sanctify and prepare themselves. I'm going to come and speak to my people. I want them to know how very much I love them." I think the people were most excited at the report from their leader, "God is going to visit us." For three days they prepared themselves. They sanctified themselves and washed their clothes and garments. They heard all of the things that were important for them to hear: Don't touch the mountain; God is holy; God is going to come and visit us.

We are not talking about standing in the outer courts and saying, "Glory to God! He is in there! There's the king in there! Let's applaud something He did." We are talking about standing face to face. A favorite chorus of mine says, "O Cloud of great glory, the Presence of God, descend now in Spirit on wings as a

37

dove." Yet the moment we get into that cloud, we begin to do whatever is comfortable for us to do. There is a place for clapping. After the Lord has spoken to us, we clap our response saying, "Yes, Lord, I heard You. Thank You for speaking to us. We are going to do it." But thank you belongs to the gate; praise belongs to the court. Worship belongs before the presence of His glory (Ps. 100).

Esther stands in the presence of the king and she is willing, as the people were willing back in Exodus. But there was a different response from the people as compared to Esther. For when God descended upon that great mountain, and it became ignited with His presence, and He spoke to them, the mountain came alive and was like fire, the Bible says.

It was a great thundering when God spoke to His people. They panicked, turned to Moses and said, "Don't you ever do that to us again. If God has something to say to us, let Him say it to you and you tell us. We can handle that."

It is a lot more comfortable to get it indirectly, isn't it? I mean, you don't really have to deal with God that way; you can deal with the person who gave you the bread, meat, or fruit. And you can say, "I didn't like the way he served it," or "It wasn't for me."

We are concerned about growing and maturing in the Lord. To the level or degree that we can feast at His table, eat with Him, fellowship with Him, delight in Him, love Him; that is the level of ministry we will have.

So Esther stands before the king, just as Moses did. That which delighted Moses was rejected by the multitude. Moses loved the presence of the Lord, entered into that cloud, and spent time with Him.

The invitation Moses received is interesting. "Dear Moses," it said, "please come up on the mountain and be there." Our response might be, "And do what?" We are so very "do" orient-ed. Some of us only see the Lord as commander in chief, and every time we report in, it is for duty. "I'll go where You want me to go; I'll do what You do what You want me to do; I have to work for You." Every time we come into His presence, He sees whatever is lacking; He knows what is ahead, and it is His pleasure to give to us everything that will be needed to the praise and honor of His name.

> *And the king loved Esther above all the women,*
> *and she obtained grace and favor in his sight more*
> *than all the virgins; so that he set the royal crown*
> *upon her head, and made her queen instead of*
> *Vashti. (2:17)*

Esther comes on the scene by the probing, prompting, and invitation of the Holy Spirit, Mordecai. She stands before his presence and he says, "All right, I will crown you because you have answered the call." I want us to look at five references concerning being crowned. Number one is Job 29:14, which tells us that we are crowned with good judgment. This is possi-bly one of the most lacking things among the family of God today. We are incapable of judging things. As time goes on and you enter a variety of ministries, whether clergy or laity, you will counsel. You may not sit behind a desk and be professional counselors, but you cannot talk with one another without an element or realm of counsel. You will find at times an individual will come to you and state their whole vantage point in a situation. Unless you are crowned with good judgment, you may make impulsive decisions, without looking into the situa-tion or hearing the other individual.

2.   Number two: Psalm 65:11 tells us that we are crowned with God's goodness. It would take us a long time to explore the goodness of God, but I challenge you to allow yourself to begin to do two things when you think about the goodness of God. One, search it out scripturally. And two, take time to meditate on how good God is, how good He has been in your life, and how He has always brought you through.

3.   Number three: In 1 Thessalonians 2:19,20, we find we are crowned with rejoicing. It is too bad that when we have, as we say in slang, "so much going for us," or God has done so much for us, that we refuse to rejoice if there is a negative on the horizon. Somehow we seem to fear that maybe people won't realize how tough things are if we rejoice. We see a person who seemingly is constantly rejoicing and praising the Lord and we say, "Well, it is obvious they don't have any problems." My friend, rejoicing is unrelated to problems. We rejoice through our problems. We receive beauty for ashes, the oil of joy for mourning, the garment of praise for the spirit of heaviness (Isa. 61:3). That happens only when you begin to praise the Lord.

I hear David say, "Bless the Lord, O my soul: and all that is within me, bless his holy name" (Ps. 103:1). I hear him saying that looking down into his soul in the days of pursuit, when he doesn't deserve the kind of life he's having to live. He says to himself, "Bless the Lord, O my soul." Maybe we could begin each day with such a statement. "Soul, you have so much to be thankful for, so much to bless the Lord for. You *will* bless the Lord, oh, my soul, and the rest of you, too. All that is within me, oh, bless His holy name." That is the crown of the Lord upon the church.

I lived through a whole season of time when the church did not know that she was crowned with rejoicing. We thought it was very spiritual to be unhappy and suffer for Jesus' sake. We taught the whole world what not to be. We often heard this statement when talking with young people about their relationship with Jesus, "After I've had my fun, I'll come to the Lord." Where did they get that idea? From us. We represented life as a long, lonely, hard, narrow way. But we did assure them that some day it would be worth it all. The Bible says, "Therefore the redeemed of the Lord shall return, and come with singing unto Zion; and everlasting joy shall be upon their head" (Isa. 51:11). That is what the Lord wants to do with us today. He wants to change us until we are crowned with rejoicing and our faces reflect Jesus.

Our next reference, 2 Timothy 4:8, tells us we are crowned with righteousness. Righteousness is a hard word to satisfactorily define. Originally the word meant right wiseness. Righteousness is imputed to us by Christ and is demonstrated as the behavior of holiness. Righteousness is the way we live. It is the way we direct our lives, our living, our thoughts. And that only comes by the holiness that is His nature, His divine attributes, the part of God himself that He puts within us when we are born again. Paul said, "Old things have passed away and all things have become new." So it is true of us. Righteousness is that with which we need to be crowned.

Our last reference is Revelation 2:10. We are crowned with life. Jesus used the words, live and life, not the words, survive and exist. I lived a great portion of my years surviving, hanging on until Jesus would come. I didn't know that when He spoke to us, He said, "Live. I am come that you might have life more abundantly than you have ever known life."

There is truth in the statement, "This world is not my home," but our interpretation has brought a wrong attitude to us. And

41

so we walk through life as if it were an endurance course, rather than understanding we are not a part of the world system. His kingdom will replace that. We have an attitude about God that He likes to put us through the sieve and see if we can survive. And then we sing, "Heavenly Father, I appreciate You."

You fathers know there is no enjoyment in seeing your children having to struggle and suffer through life. What you want for them is to keep them in the pattern of prosperity. Instead of saying, "Lord, prosper me, make me rich," say, "Lord, teach me how to live in prosperity." We need to prosper in every area so that we can come together filled with God, filled with response to Him, and enjoy His presence, and then of course that carries over. That is what we are crowned with.

Esther has done everything that she knows to do. She has obeyed the direction of the Holy Spirit. She has undergone some problems. She has had some successes: the myrrh, the spices, and the sweet odor. She has come from being weaned to utter dependence. Now she stands before the king just as she is. Is she perfect? No. Is she enough? Yes and no. She's enough as far as she can't do anything else. But she's not enough and so he says, "I will now give to you everything you need to be perfect." Don't you love the great benediction from Jude 24,25?

> Now unto him that he is able to keep you from falling, and to present you faultless before the presence of his glory with exceeding joy.
> To the only wise God our Saviour, be glory and majesty, dominion and power, both now and ever. Amen.

Far more than just words, that is a promise to us. We have a relationship that will allow God to put upon us or in this case to literally crown us with everything lacking in our lives.

Let us not ignore or refuse to believe that the problems in our lives can bring beauty for ashes. A demonstration of maturity is knowing that which is my responsibility and that which is His.

Esther stands crowned with all of this splendor, and then, as if that is not enough, let us see what else the king does.

> *Then the king made a great feast unto all his princes and his servants, even Esther's feast; and he made a release to the provinces, and gave gifts, according to the state of the king. (2:18)*

In this verse, we see Esther emerging from obscurity to stardom by direction of the king. He has invited all of his friends, the princes, and servants. And now with the crown upon Esther's head, he says "Let the feasting begin and bring Esther out and let her beauty be seen."

I believe God intends the church within the church to be His showcase. We think it is spiritual to always be hidden. It is not spiritual. The reason for being hidden is that He is not quite ready for anyone to look at you. That principle is from the bride who is veiled. Aren't you glad He veiled you? I'm glad He put a veil over me for a long period of time. And from time to time He still does. And He says to me, "You and I know where your birthmarks are, but we are not going to show them to everybody." He does that for you, too, while He is teaching you how to deal with those blemishes under that veil. He allows certain things to come into our lives so that they can perfect us. But there will come a day when He says, "Get rid of that veil and let them see your face. You don't look like you any more. You are now a reflection of Me."

43

Though seemingly simple to look at, these principles are quite another thing to appropriate. There is going to come an unveiling of the people of God. Although Esther knows where she has come from and is aware of her background which is hidden to everyone else, she dares attend the feast because the king has bidden her to come.

The second thing that we see in the feast is that he begins to give her food she has not been eating. She is not accustomed to a royal appetite. She is comfortable just being one of the commoners in the house of women.

The purpose of a banqueting table is for us to partake of the food served. Many are content to simply enjoy only the beauty of the table, without eating thereof. Our refusal to eat is due to spiritual laziness. We have become accustomed to letting others do our thinking for us. Rather than meditating for clarity and understanding, we simply refuse the food.

You are going to be eating food you have never eaten before. This is the day of increasing revelation. "But as it is written, Eye hath not seen, nor ear heard, neither have entered into the heart of man, the things which God hath prepared for them that love him" (1 Cor. 2:9).

You are being brought to the king's banquet. That means that he is going to serve you a variety of foods you have never heard of. Our questions must refer us back to our beginning. Where did Esther start? Where was the first court of women? What was there? The Word. The Word is our safety. Don't let anyone tell you that they have a revelation above and beyond the Word. We don't understand half of the half that has been told.

"And he made a release to the provinces, and gave gifts, according to the state of the king" (2:18). When the king gave a banquet or something good happened in the palace, he would diminish the taxes in the land. The reason for this was so that all the people, little people, great people, could rejoice together. That was the law according to the state of the king. Everything over which he presided, he said, "Let this not just be for us." If the church within the church truly becomes a showcase, everything we become will be a release and a blessing to the church without.

I believe that we need to understand that it is our responsibility to go back and take their hands and bless them. The more you have in God, the greater will be your blessing to everyone else. That is the whole lesson of this Scripture. They are feasting. The king says, "Not just for us. Not our little cliques. Not little groups that get together. Everything I have ought to be a blessing there in the community."

There are those who are blessed and released, but not crowned. In order to be crowned, they have come not to the person who is free, but to the person who frees the person who is free. And so our whole ministry, church, is to turn all eyes to Jesus Christ.

NOTE

He gave gifts according to the state of the king. When we think of gifts, we probably think mostly of the gifts of the Holy Spirit. And they are wonderful. Indeed the Holy Spirit himself is a gift. I will pray to the Father and He will send you the gifts from God by Jesus, the Holy Spirit. In fact, the Holy Spirit is the only gift of the Spirit. All the others that are spoken of as the nine gifts of the Holy Spirit, really aren't gifts at all. They are operations of one gift. Pick up your word study or concordance and look up the word "gift." You will find that it is a different word when it says, "the gift of the Holy Spirit" as compared to, "the gifts."

If I give my brother a shirt, that would be my gift to him. It would be his shirt. He possesses it. That is the Holy Spirit. Jesus said, "I will pray the Father, and He will give you the gift of the Holy Spirit. He will impart to you, Me." That is whom the Holy Spirit is. You know He will give Him. He is yours. But if the next week I come along and say, "May I iron that shirt for you?", that is the word that means, "there are gifts or diversities of gifts." It is the operation of that gift. It is how the Holy Spirit functions through the word of knowledge; through the word of wisdom; through faith; gifts of healing; miracles; tongues; interpretation; prophecy; discerning of spirits; the nine gifts.

It is all right to study them as gifts and separate them into the "know" gifts and the "say" gifts and the "do" gifts. We must be careful that we don't spend our whole Christian life praying for the gift of tongues or the gift of interpretation. What about the Scripture that says, 'Desire earnestly the best gift'?" I will add three words that will give you clarity, "for the occasion." When praying for the sick, we desire the gift of healing to operate which is the best gift for that occasion.

Let us talk about some of the other gifts in the Bible. Isaiah 56:5 speaks of the gift of an everlasting name. No one can take it from you. No one can erase your name from the Lamb's book of life. "I will give them an heart to know me" (Jer. 24:7). How blessed we are to have a heart to know God. Ezekiel 11:19 tells us He will give us a new spirit and a heart of flesh. He will tenderize all those hardened areas.

"I will give you rest" (Matt. 11:28). In this world in which we live, how desperately we need the gift of rest. Life is full of storms. Remember the Bible story when the disciples were in the boat? The storm came and Jesus was asleep in the back. The disciples wanted Him to rest, but they were fearful. Finally their fear turned into anger and the demand was made, "Master, carest thou not that we perish?" (Mark 4:38). Jesus immediately got up and calmed the waters and the wind — and I usually add — because it was easier than calming the disciples. What was Jesus' problem? He thought He was in His resting place. It is in the believer that He should be able to rest. But you see, we don't let Him. Every time a storm comes, we wake Him up.

What was the lesson for the disciples? I don't know what your background is, but do you remember a chorus in Sunday school that said, "With Christ in the vessel, I can smile at the storm?" That was their lesson, and they didn't learn it. Will the Lord calm the storms of your life? Yes. If He does, that will absolutely mandate another storm to come. It is necessary for you to have storm after storm, not so He can calm them but so that you can know, "If Christ is with me, it is all right; the storm isn't going to bother me." When Jesus calmed the storm, He turned to His disciples, and in Luke's account, He says, "Where was your faith?" The answer to that was, "Our faith was in the storm." They utterly believed in the power of the storm to destroy them.

We see the gift of the Holy Spirit in Luke 11:13 and the gift of peace in John 14:27. We need to see them together, for it is the Holy Spirit who is the dove of peace. Our understanding of peace is limited. We go into a cemetery and we say, "Isn't this peaceful?" It isn't peaceful. It is dead.

There is the gift of eternal life in John 10:28, and the bread of heaven in John 6:51. Your eternal life begins here on earth. We didn't always know that. We thought we could just survive here, then go to heaven and have eternal life. But the bread of heaven is to sustain you now, feed you and nourish you at the banquet we just attended, that we might grow in eternal life.

One of the most important gifts the king gives us is in Isaiah 50:4, the ability to speak words of comfort. How much we lack this ability. Have you ever desperately wanted to comfort some-one, felt inadequate to do so, and said the wrong thing? You want to say something meaningful and just end up saying, "I'm sorry." Then we run. But the Father says, "If you will come to my banquet, I will give you a gift of the ability to speak words of comfort." You will know exactly what to say and how to say it. "A word fitly spoken is like apples of gold in pictures of silver" (Prov. 25:11).

> And when the virgins were gathered together the second time, then Mordecai sat in the king's gate.
> Esther had not yet showed her kindred nor her people; as Mordecai had charged her: for Esther did the commandment of Mordecai, like as when she was brought up with him. (2:19,20)

The Holy Spirit, Mordecai, said to her, "It is not time." Esther could have had a feeling of superiority and moved out of the Holy Spirit's direction into what seemed to be right to her. The spirit of truth, who is Jesus, is a great deal more than facts. The fact was that at some time, Esther had to acknowledge her background, but that timing was not hers to determine. It is often easier for us to reveal than conceal. The spirit of truth is more concerned with the end result than exposing the situation at hand. Had Esther done this, the whole nation of Israel would have been destroyed.

James 1:5 says, "If any of you lack wisdom, let him ask of God, that giveth to all men liberally, and upbraidth not; and it shall be given him." He is not going to upbraid you for asking. I find a lack of wisdom daily in my life. Every day, I have to come back and say, "Father, grant me wisdom." Before I approach you I must say, "Lord, give me wisdom to know what to make important."

Father, grant me today Your wisdom because I come humbly and confess that I lack it. Thank You for bestowing upon me Your gifts, and for redeeming the events of my life in such a way as to make me pleasing to You. In my amazement of this, I can only delight more in You. Oh, Beloved, keep me close to You until the intimacy of that fellowship is evidenced in a display of Your beauty. Amen.

IV

Destruction of Satan and His Works

Esther 2:21-23

In those days, while Mordecai sat in the king's gate, two of the king's chamberlains, Bigthan and Teresh, of those which kept the door, were wroth, and sought to lay hand on the king Ahasuerus.

And the thing was known to Mordecai, who told it unto Esther the queen; and Esther certified the king thereof in Mordecai's name.

And when inquisition was made of the matter, it was found out; therefore they were both hanged on a tree: and it was written in the book of the chronicles before the king. (2:21-23)

Bigthan simply means, in their winepress, and Teresh means, in possession. This merely identifies them as the world. Every unbeliever is in the winepress of the world, in the possession of the world system. Any fragrance that would come from the crushing would benefit only the world. So it could be read very easily, "Two sinners wanted to kill or destroy the works of the Lord, or the king."

Joy is in the camp. Everybody is rejoicing over — let me put it in today's language — the "move of God." Churches are all benefit-

51

ing. Everybody is blessed and it is wonderful. Then suddenly we have to talk about the enemy. There is the truth.

The moment you begin to move in God in new dimensions, the certainty is that the very next thing on the scene, after you are prepared for it, will be the enemy. God will not suffer you to be tested beyond that you are able to bear (1 Cor. 10:13). Aren't you glad? But the indication is, You may be tested up to what you are able to bear. He is going to allow it. Even though I do not feel prepared, the Lord will not allow me to go through what He has not already prepared me for.

The trial of your faith is precious. To whom? Is it precious to God? I don't think so. The trial of your faith is precious *to you.* When you have been through a thing and you have come through it on your feet, you say, "I know I can do it." It moves you out of fear into faith.

Out of this glorious venture of everybody being free and singing, "Therefore the redeemed," the next thing on the scene is Mordecai saying to Esther, "There is a plot to destroy the king and all that he has brought to this land."

The immediate works of the enemy are destroyed and it would seem that everything is going to run smoothly, but we must realize that "from glory to glory" also means from battle to battle. We seem to feel that victory in one battle is winning the war.

Those who have served in the armed forces well understand that success in battle is but an opportunity to regroup and prepare for the next battle. Having done all to stand — stand therefore. And the verse goes on to describe the how. Having your loins girded about with truth, wearing the breastplate of righteousness, etc. The truth of Ephesians 6 is a needful and necessary lesson for all believers, for it teaches us to not enter the war unprepared.

There are sporadic warriors in God's army who volunteer for a specific battle. Tenacious in their stand and approach to it, they win the victory gloriously and then dismiss themselves from future responsibility. Faithfulness speaks to us of constancy. We often are weary of battling and just plain get tired of fighting self, Satan, lethargy, and much of what constitutes living. "And let us not be weary in well doing" (Gal. 6:9) is not a denial of the previous statement but an admonition to not remain weary. The remainder of the verse promises, "for in due season we shall reap, if we faint not."

We are in a war that we know we are going to win, but the Bible does not tell us how many battles we will be involved in before that comes to pass. It is no small wonder we are comforted by songs which promise, "Step by step, I'll follow Jesus. Hour by hour, I'm in His care. Day by day, He walks beside me. Through the years I know He's there."

Victories in the Old Testament were sometimes followed by periods of rest during which time new temptations had to be dealt with. In Judges 15, following a battle in which Samson slew one thousand men with the jawbone of an ass, he faces the frustration of extreme thirst and no water supply. This demanded faith in an area yet untested for him. Though his cry to God sounds more like a complaint than a request (Judg. 15:18), verse 19 shows the merciful patience of God as He uses that which is familiar to Samson to provide supernaturally that which is needed.

Battles are necessary not only to produce victories, but to increase our faith levels. Increased warfare demands increased power with God and our knowledge of Him is the source of that power.

Following what seemed to be an overemphasis on demons, many who believed themselves delivered lived in the frustration

of the recurring problem. This produced a doubting of salvation, and condemnation. We are promised in Romans 8:1,
"There is therefore now no condemnation to them which are in
Christ Jesus, who walk not after the flesh, but after the Spirit,"
yet too many believers are living in a sense of guilt. The key to
this verse is to not walk after the flesh. Galatians 5:16-21 names
specifically some of the works of the flesh. We cannot cast out
the problem by exorcising the "spirit of . . ." when the actual
problem is submitting to one's fleshly desires. Verse 17 says,
"For the flesh lusteth against the Spirit, and the Spirit against the
flesh; and these are contrary the one to the other."

This battle is a constant one in which we find ourselves
engaged and we well understand the cry of Paul, "O wretched
man that I am! who shall deliver me from the body of this
death?" (Rom. 7:24). What, then, shall we do with our feelings of
guilt and hopelessness? If it is the conviction of the Holy Spirit,
confession will alleviate guilt. If it is based on the failure of
self-efforts and introspection, we will feel condemned and that is
lasting guilt. With Paul, we cry, "I thank God through Jesus
Christ our Lord that there is deliverance for me from this body of
death." Those words spoken in faith draw the enabling power of
God to overcome self, and cause us to live victoriously.

What do we do when the Holy Spirit brings to our attention the
evil motives of someone? There are times when you just start to
get involved in business, personal, or ministerial decisions with
someone, and the Holy Spirit, our Mordecai, says, "Reject. Their
motive is impure. The thing is not right." They look like they are
there in the king's gates and they are going to bring great
wisdom, but the truth may be, they have an axe to grind.

What we should do with that information is give it to the King.
But what we often do is compare facts with one another. That is

possibly why we don't hear from the Holy Spirit more often.

The Bible says that Esther immediately went to the king and said, "The Holy Spirit tells me . . . ." Prayer is strange in that the Bible says the Lord knows what you have need of before you ask. Before you call, He will answer. Then why do we have to pray? What is so important about prayer, anyway? If the Lord knows it and then He reveals it to us, why do we have to go back and tell it to Him? Because prayer gives God the moral right to act. It releases the righteous nature of God to act on our behalf, and still be righteous and fair to the enemy.

What is prayer? It starts in the Old Testament but we see it more predominantly in the New, where consistently Jesus says to His disciples, "Pray. When you pray, pray this way." He gave them the example of prayer. And yet, even though Jesus prayed all night, when He came to the grave of Lazarus, He said, "Father, I don't need to pray this prayer. But for their sake, I'm going to pray." Was He saying prayer is not necessary? Oh, no. He was saying, "I live in a communion of prayer with the Father. I have already been sent by the Father to call Lazarus forth. I already have my orders. But I'm going to utilize prayer to build faith in the hearers."

The Lord seeks those who not only will worship Him, but He seeks those to whom He can entrust such situations as we see here, knowing that they will do the right thing with it. He wants to reveal His concerns to you. He wants to bring to you the revelation of the Holy Spirit through discernment.

I believe that the Lord is going to bring true spiritual discernment back to the church. When we discern failure of a person or the evil working of the enemy, we will know exactly what to do with it. We go immediately to the King, and say, "King, there's a threat against your workers and your work." Not just against my little church. Do you see the difference? There's a threat not just against Iverna's ministry. That would be no big deal. If I drop dead today, the family of God will go right on growing. You know what I'm saying. None of us are indispensable. Why do we take everything so personally? "They didn't like me." So what. But when there is an attack from the spirit world on the work of God, then let the family rally together and go to the King. We must be as concerned about others as we are about ourselves. They are all a part of the kingdom.

Heavenly Father, thank You that You have entrusted to me the privilege of prayer. I thank You for daily provision, health, and continuing revelation of Yourself. I praise You for Your beautiful family and pray especially for the weak, that they may be strengthened, for the fallen that they may be lifted and restored. I pray for those who have the rule over me, that they may have Your guidance, so I may live in peace. O Father, quickly perfect Your people that the knowledge of Your glory may fill all the earth. Amen.

V

Mixture and Compromise

Esther 3

After these things did King Ahasuerus promote Haman the son of Hammedatha the Agagite, and advanced him, and set his seat above all the princes that were with him. (3:1)

Haman's name means, the rager. We can see the correlation of Haman and Satan in the verse we just read. The king promoted him to a high rank, yet the spirit in him coveted the worship of God's people which prompted the diabolical plot to destroy Mordecai. Satan was the highest of the angels, promoted to a very high position, but his nature raged and for that he was later dismissed from the heavenlies.

And all the king's servants, that were in the king's gate, bowed, and reverenced Haman: for the king had so commanded concerning him. But Mordecai bowed not, nor did him reverence. (3:2)

Satan said, "I will set my throne above the throne of God. I want that worship." The most threatening position you have to the enemy is the position of worship. Far more than witnessing because he can talk the hearer out of what you are saying. Far more than anything you do, when you worship God, that is the greatest threat to Satan. His craving is that we would worship him.

> *Then the king's servants, which were in the king's gate, said unto Mordecai, Why transgressest thou the king's commandment?*
> *Now it came to pass, when they spake daily unto him, and he hearkened not unto them, that they told Haman, to see whether Mordecai's matters would stand: for he had told them that he was a Jew.*
> *And when Haman saw that Mordecai bowed not, nor did him reverence, then was Haman full of wrath.*
> *And he thought scorn to lay hands on Mordecai alone; for they had showed him the people of Mordecai: wherefore Haman sought to destroy all the Jews that were throughout the whole kingdom of Ahasuerus, even the people of Mordecai. (3:3-6)*

Peter and John are speaking with such eloquence and authority that the people are startled, because they know they are only fishermen. They are saying things so beautifully that the Bible says, "The hearers took note of them, that they had been with Jesus." There is something different about worshipers. The power of His presence increases their authority and they move in a certainty which defeats the enemy. It was evidenced in Moses, when he spent time in the presence of God. His countenance was different.

I think that is part of what "thy Father which seeth in secret himself shall reward thee openly" (Matt. 6:4) means. When you are in the secret place, you don't know that you are different. But when you come out of that place, His beauty and power are evidenced. There is power and authority that come in worship, the kind of authority that, after forty days in the presence of the Lord, allowed Moses to step down to over two million people who, in his absence had begun to worship the golden calf — a god of their own making — and demand cleansing and purification.

There is a great lack of strong leadership in the world today. Those who have been strong national leaders in the past were either devoted to God and were led by His Spirit, or to Satan and were empowered by that evil. Today there is much mixture, both in the world and in the church, and adding of human instinct, ability, and knowledge. This entrance of humanism is personified in uncertainty, vacillation, and compromise, none of which produces strong leadership.

Thank God there are men and women today who are learning to spend time in His presence and are being equipped to lead the world out of darkness and despair, into light and hope.

The purpose of the Lord is to reveal himself to the world. He has always sought to do it through a people. He will yet do it through a people. From Adam through Israel to the church, He seeks to be known. I want to do my part so that God can life us and do this through us. We must learn, then, to worship. Mordecai says, "I cannot compromise worship. I can bow to none other but God."

Do you remember Shadrach, Meshach, and Abednego? These three Hebrew children who were taken captive out of their land, became such good workers, such good servants that they were promoted to top positions in Babylon. It says to us we can serve right where we are. You can serve the Lord in the world. You can serve the church. It is no more spiritual to sweep the floor in church than it is to sweep the floor at the bank downtown

— Selah ! — if you are serving the Lord.

In the Book of Daniel, we see a story similar to Mordecai and Haman. The image of Nebuchadnezzar was put up and everyone was supposed to bow and worship. At this point Daniel said, "I cannot." Shadrach, Meschach and Abednego said, "We cannot." What are they saying? Worship can never compromise. Service can. Worship cannot.

We have had one small conflict with the enemy. We have gone to the King and immediately it is over. Do you remember the first encounter you had and how quickly it was solved? You thought every one of them would be that simple. You felt like you had the ministry of deliverance. Just as ministry grows and increases according to maturity, so do our encounters with the enemy. With increased revelation comes increased responsibility and we are given the opportunity of thwarting the plans of the enemy on a scale much larger than our own.

First Esther just deals with something that has come to her. There has been nothing face to face at all. She just heard about something and she has learned the power of prayer. Now we are beginning to enter a new dimension of dealing with the enemy.

> In the first month, that is, the month Nisan, in the twelfth year of king Ahasuerus, they cast Pur, that is, the lot, before Haman from day to day, and from month to month, to the twelfth month, that is, the month Adar.
>
> And Haman said unto king Ahasuerus, There is a certain people scattered abroad and dispersed among the people in all the provinces of thy kingdom; and their laws are diverse from all people; neither keep they the king's laws: therefore it is not for the king's profit to suffer them. (3:7,8)

Jesus said, "Satan cometh but he has nothing in me." Wouldn't it be wonderful if each of us could say that every day of our lives so that never could the accuser of the brethren go to the Lord with facts?

Haman says, "They don't even keep your laws." Can that be said of us? Or can it be said, "Thy word have I hid in mine heart, that I might not sin against thee" (Ps. 119:11)?

> *If it please the king, let it be written that they may be destroyed: and I will pay ten thousand talents of silver to the hands of those that have the charge of the business, to bring it into the king's treasuries.*
>
> *And the king took his ring from his hand, and gave it unto Haman the son of Hammedatha the Agagite, the Jews' enemy. (3:9,10)*

Why would the king allow this, or remind us again of the righteous nature of our Lord? Sometimes God allows things to happen that seem very unfair.

Why do babies die of starvation?

Why are certain countries so poverty-stricken?

Why do Christian girls ever get raped and murdered?

Why are Christian men ever beaten up?

Why do Christians lose their businesses and have them literally destroyed by the enemy?

Why do these things happen? If you fall into that trap, you will live in defeat all of your life because the only answer is, "He is Lord."

What the king is doing here is seemingly going to destroy the entire Jewish nation. He is taking his authority ring off, giving it to the enemy, and saying, "You can do anything you want to the people. Go ahead and kill them."

61

But this is not the end of the story. What seems to be today isn't the end of the book. The psalmist said, "What time I am afraid, I will trust in thee" (Ps. 56:3). The hymn writer said, "What a fellowship. What a joy divine. Leaning on the everlasting arms."

The king said to Haman, "Here is the money. And here are the people to do what seems good to you to do."

> Then were the king's scribes called on the thirteenth day of the first month, and there was written according to all that Haman had commanded unto the king's lieutenants, and to the governors that were over every province, and to the rulers of every people of every province, according to the writing thereof, and to every people after their language; in the name of king Ahasuerus was it written, and sealed with the king's ring.
>
> And the letters were sent by posts into all the king's provinces, to destroy, to kill, and to cause to perish, all Jews, both young and old, little children and women, in one day, even upon the thirteenth day of the twelfth month, which is the month Adar, and to take the spoil of them for a prey.
>
> The copy of the writing for a commandment to be given in every province was published unto all people, that they should be ready against that day.
>
> The posts went out, being hastened by the king's commandment, and the decree was given in Shushan the palace. And the king and Haman sat down to drink; but the city Shushan was perplexed. (3:12-15)

I believe the answer to chapter three is this: Things are not always what they seem. A change is going to take place. Understanding is going to come to light, and when this book ends, righteousness will have prevailed throughout all ten chapters of Esther. Truth will have been established. As we look about today, it may seem as though God has given the whole world into the hands of the enemy when in actuality it is the inheritance of the meek, the God-controlled ones.

When the church totally submits to their God, and His kingdom is established, there is not a power on earth that will not submit. Every knee shall bow, every tongue, the tongue of every devil in hell, one day shall be compelled to say, "Jesus is King of Kings and Lord of Lords." Oh, it will do them no good, but they will say it. Because that will be the day of the fulfillment of the vengeance of God against his enemy. Until then, Jesus sits allowing us to fulfill our commission.

Jesus has entrusted to the church not only the prayer, Thy kingdom come on earth, but also the responsibility of establishing that. Our position should be, "Whatsoever He saith unto you, do it." Obedience is unrelated to our ability to understand the "why" of it. It is He who knows the beginning from the end. Our part is to trust and obey.

Our witness in the past has not been supported by our actions and that has caused unbelievers to doubt us. Everything in them cries, "Oh, I wish I could believe them. I wish I could believe that Jesus would do it for me. I wish He would lift me and life me." They do not believe but they desperately want to believe. They will believe when they consistently see the appropriation of truth in us. When they can say, "They don't cheat on their taxes; they are men who love their wives; they are wives who submit to love; their children are loving, loved children; their families are solid when all others are falling apart;" instead of the picture being the same in the church as it is out there.

In verse 15, the king and Haman sat down together to drink, and the whole city was perplexed. Can we understand the king and Haman intermingling? Each time the ways of the world are brought into the church, the king and Haman are drinking together.

It is no wonder our children have little knowledge of holiness (no-add mixture), when they see the church's main concern being numbers and money. They hear us talk of love in the midst of gossip. We have become more service-oriented than worship-oriented, more concerned with the kingdom than the King.

Worship causes us to pray, "Lord cause me to hate what You hate and love what You love."

Heavenly Father, in Jesus' name I pray that You will enable me to become all You have instructed me to be. Thank You, Jesus, that Your strength is made perfect in weakness, that Your grace is sufficient, that Your power does prevail. As I walk in obedience to You, I expect to be an exact replica of You, even as I was created to be. This is too wonderful for my dreams and too possible to miss. Thank You for Your promises which are being fulfilled in my daily walk. Amen.

VI

Spirit-Directed Intercession

Esther 4:1-4

When Mordecai perceived all that was done, Mordecai rent his clothes, and put on sackcloth with ashes, and went out into the midst of the city, and cried with a loud and a bitter cry:

And came even before the king's gate: for none might enter into the king's gate clothed with sackcloth.

And in every province, whithersoever the king's commandment and his decree came, there was great mourning among the Jews, and fasting, and weeping, and wailing; and many lay in sackcloth and ashes. (4:1-3).

We open chapter four with an extreme grieving by the Holy Spirit. Mordecai is grief-stricken. There is a need for us to experience that today. Compromise has caused us to sit down with Haman and to look from a humanistic viewpoint and we have inadvertently developed an insensitivity to the Holy Spirit's concerns. It is only when we are in touch with Him that we find out what grieves Him.

65

Humanistically, we may pour our pearls out before swine, spend hours of time and energy and it will be like pouring into a bag with holes. Sympathy and a desire to change situations or people may *seem* to be a direction for prayer and many have carried a false burden from such concerns, never finding release. This is never the case when praying is directed by Mordecai.

So, Lord, teach us to pray.

May we say, "Mordecai, who, when, where, what, how?" Then the complexity of the situation and the perplexity of my own mind is released. I don't have to worry about it. If you attend a certain church, you don't have to worry about where to pay your tithe. The Bible tells you where to pay it. You pay where you eat. You don't eat in one restaurant and pay in another. Well, that releases you right there. If you can't support it, you better find out where you should be going to church. Our giving as well as our praying must be directed by the Holy Spirit.

The Holy Spirit only grieves over a situation that is potentially redemptive. The Holy Spirit not only will not waste himself, He will not waste your energies on something that He knows will never change. When He gives me His concern, I rejoice, because I know there is change ahead. I know something is going to happen.

Let's not fall into that trap that says, "If you ask a second time, you are showing a lack of faith." The Bible teaches importunity. Ask and ye shall receive means keep asking, and keep receiving. Keep seeking and keep finding. Keep knocking and it will be opened unto you. Are there ever times when the Lord says, "You don't have to ask for that any more. It is done"? Yes, when you know that He said that, then it is done. I have had promises that haven't been fulfilled that I know are done. But you know how I know it? He told me. Not people. Someone else didn't come to me and say, "It is done."

We need to know Mordecai. We need to know the Holy Spirit. We need to recognize His promptings. We need to be certain of His guidance. Our knowledge of Him comes from our obedience to the Word for He enlightens us as we obey. We have a tendency to trust Him in everyone but us, and many have been led astray by the words, "Thus saith the Lord." The Spirit and the Word are always in agreement and that is why all prophecy is either a word of confirmation or a word to be confirmed.

The Holy Spirit is not only grieved today over sin, but also over mixture and inability to discern Him. When we discover His grief, we become a part of it, and that is true intercession.

> *So Esther's maids and her chamberlains came and told it her. Then was the queen exceedingly grieved; and she sent raiment to clothe Mordecai, and to take away his sackcloth from him: but he received it not. (4:4)*

We are desirous that the Holy Spirit will share His heart, His burden, and His concern with us. But the minute He does, what do we do with it? Rather than bear the burden in prayer to God until the answer comes, we tend to talk ourselves out of it with happy songs of victory or quotation of Scripture. Esther attempted to send Him raiment to put away the grief because she was more concerned over Mordecai than the reason for his grief. Mordecai refused her offer. This means that you cannot placate the Holy Spirit.

When He is grieved, and you have shared that burden, you can't talk Him out of it. It must be borne. Let us say the Holy

Spirit begins to grieve among us and sin begins to be revealed. That may be uncomfortable for us. Or possibly another person says, "I just feel that I have to make a public confession." Or, someone begins to weep in deep sorrow for sin.

That becomes unsettling to other people. So the tendency is to get the clothes on. And we go to them and we say, "Now, the Lord doesn't want you to be grieved; the Bible says if you confess your sins, the Lord will just heal you" not realizing that the grief is part of the confession.

Do we, at times, when the Holy Spirit is dealing in our lives, excuse it by saying, "Lord, You know my frame, that I'm just dust," thus denying the possibility of change? I remind you that this scripture says, "He refused it." He said, "You won't talk Me out of it. Every time you want more from Me, we are going to deal with this very thing that you have tried to cut off."

Lord, You have seen my heart. And Holy Spirit, please don't stop dealing with me. Deal, I pray, with everything that grieves You in my life. Deal, Holy Spirit, until I come out as pure as gold and silver. Until I am the pure in heart who indeed sees God. And I thank You for Your dealings. Thank You, too, for entrusting to me Your concerns. May I be faithful to pray as You prompt me to, that I may share in Your victories. In Jesus' name, Amen.

VII

For Such a Time as This

Esther 4:5-17

*Then called Esther for Hatach, one of the king's
chamberlains, whom he had appointed to attend
upon her, and gave him a commandment to Mordecai, to know what it was, and why it was.(4:5)*

One of the beautiful benefits of being members of the body of
Christ is bearing one another's burdens. It is sad that so many of
us refuse this provision by feeling the burden is ours exclusively.
Admittedly, there are times when we are instructed to bear our
own burdens, (Gal. 6:5), but there are also times when we are
directed to share them as in Galatians 6:2. Esther began bearing her burden alone but now recognized the need to involve
Hatach, who had been assigned to her by the king for such a
time as this.

How beautiful it is to acknowledge the Lord's assignments of
pastors, prayer partners, and friends. We must learn to accept
them and release them as the King directs, rather than appoint
them to a permanency He never ordained.

*So Hatach went forth to Mordecai unto the street
of the city, which was before the king's gate.*

And Mordecai told him of all that had happened unto him, and of the sum of the money that Haman had promised to pay to the king's treasuries for the Jews, to destroy them.

Also he gave him the copy of the writing of the decree that was given at Shushan to destroy them, to shew it unto Esther, and to declare it unto her, and to charge her that she should go in unto the king, to make supplication unto him, and to make request before him for her people.

And Hatach came and told Esther the words of Mordecai. (4:6-9)

Before accepting or sharing the burden of the Holy Spirit, personal inventory must be taken to determine whether we are part of the problem. We must resolve that part in order that we may become part of the solution. Neither Esther nor Hatach are a part of the problem and thus each is committed to work together with Mordecai in bringing the solution. The Holy Spirit, acknowledging this, reveals the problem through Hatach to Esther.

All the king's servants, and the people of the king's provinces, do know, that whosoever, whether man or woman, shall come unto the king into the inner court, who is not called, there is one law of his to put him to death, except such to whom the king shall hold out the golden sceptre, that he may live: but I have not been called to come unto the king these thirty days.

And they told to Mordecai Esther's words. (4:11,12)

70

The price is being weighed. Esther says, "I'd like to be a part of your concern, but do you realize it could cost me my life?" The Holy Spirit is searching today for people who will make eternal commitments. This is why the Word encourages us to count the cost, lest we become partially involved and fail to complete the task bringing shame both to us and His kingdom as illustrated in Luke 14. If our goals begin and end with self, we will not be counted among the overcomers who loved not their lives unto the death (Rev. 12:11). It is only when our vision encompasses the whole world and the establishing of His kingdom that we can make such a commitment.

What is this commitment? It is a determination to die to self — self lusts, goals, desires — and to live the resurrected life by the power of and under the direction of the Spirit of God. Our entrance into the King's presence demands death of self, but not destruction as we fear.

> *Then Mordecai commanded to answer Esther,*
> *Think not with thyself that thou shalt escape in the*
> *king's house, more than all the Jews. (4:13)*

Mordecai reminds Esther that her concern must go beyond herself, and that her place of prominence is but a tool to bring salvation to her people. God help us to understand that rather than being put in a prominent place because of some consecration or good that I have done, God often places me there to fulfill His purpose. What happens to His church, whether persecution or judgment, affects us as we are a part of the whole. The five-fold ministry is the gift of Jesus to the church for the perfecting of the saints. Revelation and truth, when given and received, result in blessing for both giver and receiver. That is the economy of God.

> *For if thou altogether holdest thy peace at this time, then shall there enlargement and deliverance arise to the Jews from another place; (4:14a)*

Mordecai is saying, "Deliverance is going to come to the church with or without you." We are not indispensable, yet each person is important. We may refuse God's opportunity to be involved in His victory thus relinquishing personal reward of maturity and blessing but we will not thwart the ultimate intention of God for His people.

> *But thou and thy father's house shall be destroyed: and who knoweth whether thou art come to the kingdom for such a time as this? (4:14b)*

We come to that for which Esther has been prepared. She is now called upon to utilize her knowledge of and influence with the king for the preserving of a nation. Oh, may we learn to be sensitive to the Holy Spirit so that we may know when our time to be involved has come.

Now Esther must bear her burden alone. The specifics of this moment may never be repeated. The opportunity is now, yet the choice is hers. She may choose to wait and hope for another opportunity or move as the Holy Spirit is prompting. The taking up of our cross daily and following Jesus demands commitment to a walk of daily decisions. It is comforting to know that when we err in making decisions, we may know the correction of the Holy Spirit. In Acts 16, Paul decided to go to Bithynia, "but the Spirit suffered them not" (v.7). Now without specific direction, he went to Troas and waited. That there was a need for his ministry in Bithynia is true, but he was not directed there at that time. Paul's willingness to heed the direction of the Holy Spirit opened to him new vision, and he was made to realize Macedonia was open for such a time as this.

We may feel unfulfilled while doing good in the kingdom. We may even be preaching, teaching, or serving in a place we feel needs what we have to offer yet we lack personal satisfaction. This may be because we are self-appointed and have missed the higher appointment by the King which would have produced total fulfillment, not merely success.

> *Then Esther bade them return Mordecai this answer,*
> *Go, gather together all the Jews that are present in Shushan, and fast ye for me, and neither eat nor drink three days, night or day: I also and my maidens will fast likewise; and so will I go in unto the king, which is not according to the law: and if I perish, I perish. (4:15,16)*

First of all, we begin to see the burden is accepted. Are we going to accept the burden? Are we going to accept the realization that we may have been born into the kingdom for such a time as this? Then we will need to know our lives will have to make a difference. We need to know, then, that God has brought us through this preparation, and every place we go, we will make a difference just because we are there and we have accepted the burden.

All too often we see intercession as only words of prayer. Many times intercession is standing in the gap for someone, in other words, being strength in their time of weakness, providing food for the hungry, rather than just promising to pray about it.

Secondly, Esther takes only what is her part to do. Rather than seeing herself as a superstar, Esther recognizes that she is but one instrument in this great cause. She called upon all the others involved in this concern to do what they must do also.

For too long, we have felt that the victories of our church depended wholly upon the pastor rather than accepting the responsibility of preparing ourselves to receive that which God has given him to share. When anointed clergy and anointed laity are knitted together for the purpose of pleasing the King, there is scripture fulfilled and the King's delight expressed. "All my springs are in thee" (Ps. 87:7).

Prior to every move of God, there has been a demand for preparation. Only those who have completed the preparation receive the revelation.

Esther calls for a three-day fast and declares her personal willingness to be involved, even to die, if necessary. While Esther calls for the fast, it is Mordecai who births the desire in the people to fulfill it.

Self or people-directed fasting provides little more than obedience and self-discipline. God-directed fasting adds to this spiritual victory. "So Mordecai went his way, and did according to all that Esther had commanded him" (4:17).

Beloved Father, I do not want to hold my life dear unto myself. I pray that You will grant me vision and insight into Your divine intention for Your kingdom. Grant that I may be found worthy to share Your concern, and give me the wisdom to know when that burden must be borne alone or shared with another. I ask that the Holy Spirit

74

will be so in control of my life that I will not miss your open doors nor mistake the need for the call. Thank You, Jesus, for teaching me to pray with the understanding of doing my part in the fulfill-ment. In this understanding, I pray, Thy kingdom come. Amen.

VIII

Walking in Spiritual Authority

Esther 5

*Now it came to pass on the third day, that Esther
put on her royal apparel, and stood in the inner
court of the king's house, over against the king's
house: and the king sat upon his royal throne in
the royal house, over against the gate of the house.
(5:1)*

The burden has been accepted, assumed, and shared, no
matter what the cost. It is seldom enough just to pray. There are
some things that we have to become involved in.

The order has been given; the time is right. Now Esther must
see the king, but she does not send for him. She goes to where
he is. For too long, rather than rise to higher ground, we have
endeavored to bring the King down to where we live. It is no
wonder that the Word consistently speaks of growing and coming up higher, for it is not in the outer court that the King dwells.
Esther is seeking a relationship with the king, one she has not
had before, one of authority.

Though instructed that we may come boldly before His
throne, isn't it sad to see people who spend the first five minutes

of their prayer time apologizing to the Lord? "Lord, I know I'm not what I should be. I really shouldn't be coming to You. And Lord, I wouldn't blame You if You didn't want me."

How embarrassing it would be if our children were like that with us. "I don't deserve this, and I really shouldn't even bother you." You just want to stop them and say, "Say it!" There comes a time when the Lord says, "What is it that you want?"

Esther realizes that she is going to come before the king, and so she puts on her royal apparel. There is a lesson in the words, "put off" and "put on" in the New Testament. Put off the old and put on the new. Put on or add to your faith, virtue, and to virtue, knowledge, and so on (2 Pet. 1:5-8). All of these are your royal apparel. Begin to live this way and you will come closer to Him.

> *And it was so, when the king saw Esther the queen standing in the court, that she obtained favour in his sight: and the king held out to Esther the golden sceptre that was in his hand. So Esther drew near, and touched the top of the sceptre. (5:2)*

It is when the king saw Esther moving from the court to the inner chamber, that the grace-filled sceptre of acceptance was extended toward her and she touched it, acknowledging this acceptance. As long as we are bound in the bonds of self-depreciation and unwillingness to trust our relationship with Jesus, we will never be prepared for the next question by the King.

> *Then said the king unto her, What wilt thou, queen Esther? and what is thy request? it shall be even given thee to the half of the kingdom.*

78

And Esther answered, If it seem good to the king, let the king and Haman come this day unto the banquet that I have prepared for him.

Then the king said, Cause Haman to make haste, that he may do as Esther hath said. So the king and Haman came to the banquet that Esther had prepared. (5:3-5)

There she stood in the inner court. "He that dwelleth in the secret place of the most High shall abide under the shadow of the Almighty" (Ps. 9:1) How wonderful it is to know that there is an inner court. There is a place of fellowship where we can not only come and visit, but where we can dwell.

Now the sceptre is lowered and the king says, "Come into my presence." She stands in his presence and he says, "What do you want?"

Do you know that many Christians today would be absolutely frustrated by that question? We evade it with "Whatever You want for me, Lord. Thy will be done. Whatever You don't like, take out; whatever You see missing, put it in."

There comes a time in our Christian maturity, when the Lord can entrust us with the question, "What do you want?" Your inability to answer that question may be a revelation to you, that you are without a goal. Ask Him, "Lord, what do You want for me?" Search His Word and find some answers. Are you living beneath your privileges? Are you fearful of the call of God that you sense upon your life?

"Well, I just can't live it." Can't or won't? You are the only one who can answer that. If you can't, I have good news for you. He will enable you. If you won't, I have bad news for you. You are in trouble.

Esther said, "I want very much for you and Haman to come to a banquet which I will prepare." That statement wouldn't be quite so strange if she would simply say, "I want you to come to a banquet." So let's look at that first. Is she trying to program him like we unfortunately learn to do in our culture? Is that what Esther is doing? Is she trying to, as we say, "butter him up" and get him all soft and pliable so that, at the right moment, she can say, "Now, here's what I want you to do"? Not at all.

In Ezekiel 44, let us look at the story of two priesthoods. The general attitude of the priesthood was this: Whatever pleases the people, we will do it. For years it seemed like everybody got by with it. Finally the Lord said, "Ezekiel, I want you to say some things to my priests. These priests who have compromised shall be priests in my sanctuary." What a beautiful picture of mercy. He says, "They shall be priests, but they shall not come near unto Me. They may not eat at my table. They may not minister unto Me."

This is the picture of every person who has a legalistic position with Christ. Many people hear this, "If you confess your sins, He will forgive you and you will go to heaven." And they confess their sins, they are forgiven, and they are going to heaven. And that is the whole of their relationship. They have a legal right to go to heaven.

God said to Ezekiel, "They may minister unto the people. They can offer the sacrifices. They can take the sacrifices for sin. They can talk about sin and salvation. They can deal with the people there. They can speak to the people of my laws. But they may not come near unto Me."

What a penalty. And then He says, "Ezekiel, there were also the sons of Zadok." Interestingly, Zadok means, righteousness. Zadok was the priest who was faithful to David when his son came in to usurp the throne, and David had to escape. As he was running, he turned around and saw Zadok, the priest. He said, "Where are you going?"

Zadok said, "David, I am yours. My heart is with you."

David said, "Oh, I appreciate that, but listen. I need you to stay here more than I need you to come with me."

And Zadok remained faithful and true to David, who is to us a type of Jesus. In other words, there were those who lived in righteousness and it didn't matter to them what people thought.

He said, "The sons of Zadok shall come near unto Me. They shall eat and feast with Me at the table of shewbread. They shall know my presence. They shall fellowship with Me."

Now, at first glance, it would seem more useful for us to not be the sons of Zadok. The Bible says that the priests can minister to people, make the sacrifices, and have charge at the gates. Then there are the sons of Zadok and it looks like all that they do is come in and just praise the Lord, and love the Lord, and be spiritual.

Not true. What this says is, "These who are at my fellowship table, they shall first come to Me and minister unto Me." Are you a minister unto the Lord, or are you a minister on His behalf? Is ministry unto Him limited to praise, fellowship, communion, singing, magnifying, glorifying, exalting, and worshiping Him? Is that where it ends? Those who were the sons of Zadok did all of this ministry unto the Lord; then they came out from the holy place unto the people.

If they are both taking sacrifices from the people and being priests unto the people, why is it so important to minister unto God first? Because those who could not come near the Lord could only minister law. Those who came into His presence first and then went out to the people, ministered His life.

81

What kind of minister do you want to be? You can have all the facts and spend the rest of your life giving the facts to people, but it will not change lives. It may change behavior. But if we stand in His presence and become filled with Him, when we come out, the Word of the Lord will be truth and power and sharp as a two-edged sword. It will be tendered with grace, love, life, and hope. Lives will be changed as the Word goes forth.

There are two key verses in Ezekiel 44:23,24, where Ezekiel says of the sons of Zadok: "They shall teach my people the difference between the holy and profane . . . And in controversy they shall stand in judgment, and they shall judge it according to my judgments."

Profane in the Bible, in the Old Testament, means, that which is unconsecrated. It doesn't mean taking the Lord's name in vain. It means, anything that is not consecrated unto God, or "They shall teach my people the difference between the necessary and the unnecessary." That is what the church is crying to know today. What is important? What should our focus be? Where should our emphasis be? He says, "My sons of Zadok will teach you."

The complexity is that Esther not only invites the king to her banquet, she also invites Haman, the rager, who represents the devil here. Why should she do that? The easiest way to unmask the enemy is to bring him into worship. Don't venture onto his territory to deal with him. Let him venture on God's territory. The enemy, Haman, is thrilled to be invited. He believes it to be an opportunity to fulfill his own purposes.

> *And the king said unto Esther at the banquet of*
> *wine, What is thy petition? and it shall be granted*
> *thee: and what is thy request? even to the half of*

> *the kingdom it shall be performed.*
>
> *Then answered Esther, and said, My petition and my request is;*
>
> *If I have found favour in the sight of the king, and if it please the king to grant my petition, and to perform my request, let the king and Haman come to the banquet that I shall prepare for them, and I will do to morrow as the king hath said. (5:6-8)*

Why didn't Esther just come out and say it? What is she building up to?

She says, "The more I am in His presence, the more authority is being meted out to me."

The more I learn to give to Him and worship Him and minister unto Him, the greater my own capacities to receive the authority of God.

And she repeats the invitation for them both to attend a second banquet.

> *Then went Haman forth that day joyful and with a glad heart: but when Haman saw Mordecai in the king's gate, that he stood not up, nor moved for him, he was full of indignation against Mordecai.*
>
> *Nevertheless Haman refrained himself: and when he came home, he sent and called for his friends, and Zeresh his wife.*
>
> *And Haman told them of the glory of his riches, and the multitude of his children, and all the things wherein the king had promoted him, and how he had advanced him above the princes and servants of the king.*

> *Haman said moreover, Yea, Esther the queen*
> *did let no man come in with the king unto the*
> *banquet that she had prepared but myself; and to*
> *morrow am I invited unto her also with the king.*
> *(5:9-12)*

Satan is not omniscient. Haman doesn't understand why Esther is inviting him in. Satan does not know everything. He is not equal with God. He only knows what God has allowed him to know. He is still convinced he can win, and we give him far too much credit. We credit him with knowing every thought we have. He cannot read your mind; but he can project things into it. He doesn't know what you do with them until you speak.

Haman is convinced that he has really conquered authority. The devil is convinced today that he has won. The majority numerically and financially seems to govern everything that exists in our world with the utilization of his tactics.

God's promise in this situation is, "Greater is he that is in you, than he that is in the world" (1 John 4:4).

I may not understand the Lord's battle strategy, or how He wins with a minority of three hundred men, lamps, pitchers, and trumpets, but the lesson of Gideon is proof that He does (Judg. 7). All He asks is our willingness and obedience. He will do the rest.

> *Yet all this availeth me nothing, so long as I see*
> *Mordecai the Jew sitting at the king's gate.*
> *Then said Zeresh his wife and all his friends*
> *unto him, Let a gallows be made of fifty cubits*
> *high, and to morrow speak thou unto the king that*
> *Mordecai may be hanged thereon: then go in mer-*

rily with the king unto the banquet. And the thing pleased Haman; and he caused the gallows to be made. (5:13-14)

The same spirit that is evidenced in Haman and his family was demonstrated at Calvary. This spirit tries hopelessly to destroy Christ and all who will worship Him. Every effort thus made becomes the building of the gallows on which Satan, himself must ultimately be destroyed.

O Righteous Father, how I thank You for sending Jesus that I might have access to Your presence. Forgive me for my willingness to stagnate, to remain in the blessings of the past, to be spiritually impotent. Grant that I may behold You in Your beauty and learn to fellowship with You where You are. May my desire to live in Your authority never be for self-exaltation, rather that I may become a vessel of honor as it pleases the King. Thank You, Father, that through Jesus Christ I have been delivered from the power of the enemy and all of his intentions for me are made void through Jesus Christ. In You and in this do I rejoice daily. Amen.

IX

Honor to Whom Honor Is Due

Esther 6

Divine destiny, rather than situational circumstance is evidenced in this chapter. Just as judgment is often postponed, and promises are unfulfilled in our time schedule, so it is that God has times for revealing people and situations. About eight years have passed since Bigthan and Teresh's plot to destroy the king was reported and thwarted by Mordecai. It is now God's time for recognition.

One sleepless night the king requested the records of the chronicles to read. He began to read about Bigthana and Teresh and how someone had reported that they were going to kill the king. He began to wonder if he ever rewarded that man. The next day, he inquired as to who was out there in the court. The king was told that Haman was in the court and he said, "Bring Haman in. I want to talk to him." When Haman came in, the king asked, "What do you think ought to be done to a man who had really saved my life?"

Haman sees HAMAN in big letters. So he says, "I will tell you what I think. I think you ought to bring in the royal apparel which you used to wear, and the horse that you used to ride, and the royal crown that sat upon your head. And I think the apparel ought to be put on the man whom the king delighteth to honour." In his mind, Haman is already wearing it. "And I think you ought to put him on horseback and take him through the streets of the city and proclaim before him, 'Thus shall it be done to the man whom the king delighteth to honour.'"

The idea pleased the king and it became his command.

So Haman readied the apparel and the horse, and he prepared to accept the glory and honor for himself. The king then requested him to summon Mordecai as the one to whom this honor was due. A gradual revelation of Haman to Haman is unfolding. You will see it as we go along.

Haman didn't have any options. He took the apparel and the horse and arrayed Mordecai. All the glory Satan wants, God is going to demand that he give back to us. He brought Mordecai on horseback through the streets of the city, and proclaimed before him, "This is the way you will be treated, any one of you who honour the king." But he is thinking, "Oh, if I could just kill him!"

That reminds me of "the devil, as a roaring lion, walketh about, seeking whom he may devour" (1 Peter 5:8). MAY! He could devour any of us. He is capable. He has greater power than we have. But he *may* not. He is not given permission from the One who owns him. It is like Daniel in the lions' den. How do you think those lions felt? "If we could only get our mouths open. Just one gulp!" You see, that is the way the devil feels about you and me, "Just let me have one bite!" The Lord says, "No, I'll let you have one roar." The threat of that sound causes us to hasten into the presence of Jesus where we have found refuge oft times before.

> And Mordecai came again to the king's gate. But
> Haman hasted to his house, mourning, and hav-
> ing his head covered. (6:12)

Haman retreats to those of his family, but he will find no comfort there, for when judgment is at hand, God will cause the Spirit of truth to be spoken. From the mouth of God, through the voice of Zeresh, Haman's wife, comes the prophecy of his fall.

> And Haman told Zeresh his wife and all his
> friends every thing that had befallen him. Then
> said his wise men and Zeresh his wife unto him, If
> Mordecai be of the seed of the Jews, before whom
> thou hast begun to fall, thou shalt not prevail
> against him, but shalt surely fall before him. (6:13)

His supporters' inability to comfort, the true word of judgment declared, and the revelation of himself to himself nearly com-pleted, have left Haman defensively awaiting orders from the king.

> And while they were yet talking with him, came
> the king's chamberlains, and hasted to bring
> Haman unto the banquet that Esther had pre-
> pared. (6:14)

While Haman has lost hope that the king will honor him and may be questioning the original invitation from Esther, he has no opportunity now to refuse attendance, and is escorted there by the king's chamberlains.

Almighty God, mighty in power and in justice, teach me to trust in Your character and to not judge in the circumstances at hand. Your promises are yea and amen, and the delay of the fulfillment never negates the promise. You have said I shall reap in due season if I faint not. I seek not Your rewards that I may be seen of men, rather that men may see my good works and Your blessings upon me and give glory unto You. Forgive my self-seeking and desire for credit for I have learned that the applause of men produces no lasting effect. In my life, Lord, be glorified. In Jesus' name, Amen.

X

The Word of the King

Esther 7

So the king and Haman came to banquet with Esther the queen.

And the king said again unto Esther on the second day at the banquet of wine, What is thy petition, queen Esther? and it shall be granted thee: and what is thy request? and it shall be performed, even to the half of the kingdom.

Then Esther the queen answered and said, If I have found favour in thy sight, O king, and if it please the king, let my life be given me at my petition, and my people at my request:

For we are sold, I and my people to be destroyed, to be slain and to perish. But if we had been sold for bondmen and bondwomen, I had held my tongue, although the enemy could not countervail the king's damage. (7:1-4)

"Where the word of a king is, there is power: and who may say unto him, What doest thou?" (Eccles. 8:4).

The Word of God and the God of the Word are one, which is why it is impossible for Him to lie. The Bible is not merely the

Word inspired, rather it is the expression of God who declares it shall not return unto Him void. We can neither add to nor take from without penalty.

Recognizing this, Queen Esther must have been filled with delightful anticipation as she is promised her petition will be granted. It is incredible that we have a variety of verses with this same promise yet rather than expecting answers, we doubt. Ask, and ye shall receive. We ask without really expecting to receive. Have we become so accustomed to the miracles and blessings of God that they are taken for granted?

Perhaps the many voices all declaring, "Thus saith the Lord" have dulled our hearing and encouraged our doubting. If Esther does not trust the word of the king, she will have made a horrendous mistake in inviting him to the banquet and indeed her own life will be in jeopardy. It is the word of the king that will make the difference.

In our relationship with the King, we recognize His lordship and in that recognition there is no fear of exposing any area of our lives to His searchlight. The redemptive grace of God and the power of the blood of Jesus Christ so cover the negatives of our past, they leave only the true enemy vulnerable and exposed to the righteous anger of God. Esther's cry is, "If it please the king, deliver me from the evil one."

> Then the king Ahasuerus answered and said unto Esther the queen, Who is he, and where is he, that durst presume in his heart to so do?
> And Esther said, The adversary and enemy is this wicked Haman. Then Haman was afraid before the king and the queen. (7:5-6)

"Submit yourselves therefore to God. Resist the devil" (James 4:7). Esther has done this and the exposing of Haman has caused him to fear before the king and queen. Esther has found strength in the presence of the king and that strength has become threatening to the enemy whose usual tactics are to move in areas of weakness.

God wants us to be strong in the Lord that instead of fearing the enemy, the enemy will fear us. It was the presence of Jesus that caused the demons to cry out for permission to enter the herd of swine (Matt. 8:28-33). It is still His presence in us which causes evil to submit and flee before the face of the king.

> *And the king arising from the banquet of wine in his wrath went into the palace garden: and Haman stood up to make request for his life to Esther the queen; for he saw that there was evil determined against him by the king.*
>
> *Then the king returned out of the palace garden into the place of the banquet of wine; and Haman was fallen upon the bed whereon Esther was. Then said the king, Will he force the queen also before me in the house? As the word went out of the king's mouth, they covered Haman's face. (7:7-8)*

In his fear, Haman fell down. The king stepped into the palace garden in wrath. Haman stood up to make a request for his life to the queen, and fell down onto the bed where Esther was. As he is making a plea for his life, the king returns and pronounces judgment on the thing at hand. Nothing the enemy can do is right. He has no defense. There is nothing to say back to the king. It isn't a matter of his guiltlessness; he is guilty. If he thought forcing her would do it, he would have forced her.

The enemy never moves against strength. The enemy always moves against weakness. When you are overtired; when you are sick; when you are depressed; when you have problems in other areas; the enemy comes immediately. And if he can't get you there, he finds the weakness of sympathy. That is why we must constantly pray, "Lord, help me to love what You love and hate what You hate and let me not be deceived by the enemy."

> *And Harbonah, one of the chamberlains, said before the king, Behold also, the gallows fifty cubits high, which Haman had made for Mordecai, who had spoken good for the king, standeth in the house of Haman. Then the king said, Hang him thereon.*
>
> *So they hanged Haman on the gallows that he had prepared for Mordecai. Then was the king's wrath pacified. (7:9,10)*

The effect of the enemy's power over the believer was destroyed on resurrection day. But the word of the King promises a day yet to come when the bottomless pit becomes the gallows on which the enemy is destroyed and God's judgment is fulfilled in His righteousness.

O Glorious King, I delight in Your Word as I delight myself in You. Thank You for Your love which has released me from pretense and shame. Thank You for covering me with Your robe of righteousness that I no longer am clothed in filthy rags. I rejoice in Your power to subdue the enemy and in Your power to change and sustain my life. Grant that I may be so one with You doing only that which pleases You, that I may become a living demonstration of Your glory, causing the enemy to flee as I worship You in Spirit and in truth. Amen.

XI

Restoration

Esther 8

On that day did the king Ahasuerus give the house of Haman the Jews' enemy unto Esther the queen. And Mordecai came before the king; for Esther had told what he was unto her.

And the king took off his ring, which he had taken from Haman, and gave it unto Mordecai. And Esther set Mordecai over the house of Haman. (8:1,2)

In our identifying with Esther, we rejoice to see the king give the house of Haman to her. Everything which belonged to the enemy, the Lord has taken out of his hand and offered to the church. Many of us have not yet received it. For example, the creative arts have been snatched by the enemy. It is time for the church to take them back. I believe that inventive abilities and inventive powers which belong to the church were taken by the world system — because the church mishandled and misused them — but were provisionally restored at Calvary.

The Lord wants to return the inventive capacity to godly men and women, not only the creative arts and inventive minds, but wisdom. We need to understand that what the world has out there is really given to us.

Dancing belongs to the church. Dancing has always been an expression of joy which was coupled with feasting in the Bible. Because the enemy could not talk us out of it, he displayed the counterfeit of it sensually and with every perversion and filth that so represents him. When there was more counterfeit dancing than real, God's people, fearing they would be identified with the dancing of the world, gave it up. But in this new day of restoration, God's people are beginning to dance once more.

The enemy says, "This world is mine."

God says "It is the inheritance of my people."

What will we do with it? The king took the ring off and he gave it to Mordecai. The ring signified authority. The holder of it could speak in his name, being assured that the king's power supported all that was said.

Esther has all of the possessions of Haman, but Mordecai has all the authority of the king.

Some years ago when in South Carolina, I was taken to a slave market. I had never been able to understand slavery because I grew up in California and Oregon, and it was foreign to my thinking. I could not relate to one human being selling another human being to a third human being. I viewed the place where the auctioneer stood and above that was another level where the slaves were offered. Facing these two platforms were long sheds where the people stood and did their bidding. In my attempt to get the feel of those times long ago, I had a mental vision. I saw myself as the auctioneer. And I was preaching what you might identify as an acceptable evangelical sermon.

I said, "Ladies and gentlemen, here He is. His name is Jesus. If you have a sickness, He will heal it. If you have a marriage problem, He will solve it. If you have financial difficulties, He will bring His wisdom to you." I heard myself say, "Turn around, Jesus."

And I saw Him slowly turn around in obedience to me. People have asked me, "What did He look like?" I said, "He looked like the paintings that I have seen so that I would recognize Him."

Then I made my final plea to the audience by saying, "It has all been paid. All you have to do is take Him home."

The vision faded, and very honestly I didn't comprehend its full meaning. I remember feeling some tears on my cheek, and I asked that I might be taken back to my hotel. By the time I got to my room, I well understood my vision. I found my key, got inside, threw my purse and coat on the bed, and fell down beside it. Somehow I didn't feel low enough, so I prostrated myself on that filthy hotel carpet. You see, I realized I had the whole thing reversed. It is Iverna who should have been on the slave block, being directed out to the needs of the people by the Holy Spirit, who is in control of me. Do you see the difference? No one has ever worshiped a servant. He is not your servant. You are His. He is King Jesus. High, holy, omniscient, omnipotent, omnipresent. He is Almighty God, Jehovah. When we see this, we worship Him.

In Esther 8, everything is given to her. The New Testament says, "All things are yours. I give you My glory. I give you everything the Father has given to Me."

"And Esther set Mordecai over the house of Haman" (8:2). I must set the Holy Spirit over everything that has been given to me. I am incapable, without Him, of knowing how and where to share my gifts.

It would seem that Esther has everything she wants including safety for her people.

And Esther spake yet again before the king, and fell down at his feet, and besought him with tears to put away the mischief of Haman the Agagite, and his device that he had devised against the Jews. (8:3)

Jesus said, "You have not because you ask not. Ask largely, ask, ask, ask."

She fell down at his feet. Worship precedes the request evidencing humility and unselfishness for she has received much for herself. Yet because her vision is far-reaching, request must follow request until the entire kingdom is restored.

"She besought him with tears to put away the mischief of Haman the Agagite, and his device that he had devised against the Jews." Esther said, "Haman is dead, but his mischief lives on." The ways of the enemy exist in your life even after you have been freed from the enemy. There is still that hanging on of the old habit patterns, trends, and pressures of the world.

Esther said, "I am not content just to know that the devil has been destroyed that he has no place in me; I want even his system, the petitions that he has put out, and the laws that challenge me to be broken."

There is a similar cry in the church today against worldliness and humanism which is the diabolical doctrine of man as his own god. First John 3:8 tells us that Jesus came to destroy the works of the devil.

Then the king held out the golden sceptre toward Esther. So Esther arose, and stood before the king. (8:4)

The bride, whenever the sceptre is lowered, will always respond to the presence of the king. May we never be too preoccupied to respond to His invitation. We can become immune to the nudgings of the Holy Spirit by consistently ignoring them. It is difficult for us to take time to stop. The veil has been rent in twain, the access road has been completed, and the sceptre has been lowered. Ours is only to respond.

> *If it please the king, and if I have found favour in his sight, and the thing seem right before the king, and I be pleasing in his eyes, let it be written to reverse the letters devised by Haman the son of Hammedatha the Agagite, which he wrote to destroy the Jews which are in all the king's provinces: (8:5)*

Esther now stands before the king, fearless, knowing that that which he has given is hers and will not be withdrawn. She trusts that her request will be granted and her prayer now becomes more specific. Following repentance and cleansing, the bestowing of gifts, the falling at his feet and worshiping, the flowing of tears both of delight and concern, there is a time for the believer to stand before the King and make his petitions known. This is the boldness we are instructed to possess as we enter into His presence (Heb. 10:19). Esther's boldness was balanced by her desire to please the king.

> *For how can I endure to see the evil that shall come to my people? or how can I endure to see the destruction of my kindred? (8:6)*

This is the heart cry of the bride we must identify with, for there can be no unity in the church until there is an identifying of each member to each other. This unity will enable us to fulfill the law of the New Testament summarized in 1 John 3:18: "My little children, let us not love in word, neither in tongue; but in deed and in truth." This love becomes the key and opens the door to true intercession, and releases us from the concern of petty differences.

> *Then the king Ahasuerus said unto Esther the queen and to Mordecai the Jew, Behold, I have given Esther the house of Haman, and him they have hanged upon the gallows, because he laid his hand upon the Jews.*
> *Write ye also for the Jews, as it liketh you, in the king's name, and seal it with the king's ring: for the writing which is written in the king's name and sealed with the king's ring, may no man reverse. (8:7,8)*

We have seen the restoration of gifts, of our inheritance, of sharing the heart of God for His presence. Now we are to see a restoration of authority.

While we may enjoy the words, power and authority, we may be reticent to accept the responsibility that accompanies them. Many would prefer to have the King do it all for us, rather than to have to be involved ourselves.

All that has preceded has been preparation for this glorious restoration of power. Esther has given the Holy Spirit ultimate control over all she possesses. Her petitions have revealed her concern for the whole family of God and she may now be trusted to seal with the king's ring. One day the voice of the church will no longer be ignored for that which is sealed with the King's ring, may no man reverse.

> *Then were the king's scribes called at the time in the third month, that is, the month Sivan, on the three and twentieth day thereof; and it was written according to all that Mordecai commanded unto the Jews, and to the lieutenants, and the deputies and rulers of the provinces which are from India unto Ethiopia, an hundred twenty and seven provinces, unto every province according to the writing thereof, and unto every people after their language, and to the Jews according to their writing, and according to their language.*
>
> *And he wrote in the king Ahasuerus' name, and sealed it with the king's ring, and sent letters by posts on horseback, and riders on mules, camels, and young dromedaries:*
>
> *Wherein the king granted the Jews which were in every city to gather themselves together, and to stand for their life, to destroy, to slay, and to cause to perish, all the power of the people and province that would assault them, both little ones and women, and to take the spoil of them for a prey. (8:9-11)*

Prior to this time it was unlawful for the Jews to retaliate no matter what was done to them because they were held captive. If you are serving the enemy, you have no right to retaliate. But when the time comes that you are so given over to the Holy Spirit, that God Almighty, God the Father, God the Son, and God the

Spirit have total possession of you, then you may serve notice on the enemy.

We have been given the power to stand for life. We have been given the power to cause to perish all of the powers of the peoples and the provinces that would assault. We are to take whatever is leftover for us. In other words, the victory belongs to us.

Lessons being learned today in the body of Christ teach us that gentlemen are having to learn to identify with being members of the bride, while ladies are having to learn what it means to be sons of God and in His army. When we put the two together, we understand that there are times when He says, "Come, stand before Me, and worship." It is foolish to war when He says, "Worship." There are other times when He says, "Go forth and conquer," and we would be unsuccessful and disobedient were we to just stand and worship. So we are the bride of Christ prepared at any moment to do anything in the name of the King. His bride wears combat boots.

> Upon one day in all the provinces of king Ahasuerus, namely upon the thirteenth day of the twelfth month, which is the month Adar.
> The copy of the writing for a commandment to be given in every province was published unto all people, and that the Jews should be ready against that day to avenge themselves on their enemies. (8:12,13)

The word has gone out. The king has commanded the Jews to be involved that they may (v.11) stand for their life, destroy, slay, and cause to perish all the powers that would assault them. Now the task is theirs.

*So the posts that rode upon mules and camels
went out, being hastened and pressed on by the
king's commandment. And the decree was given
at Shushan the palace. (8:14)*

There have been many before us who have served notice to
the enemy, and that notice has been ignored as Satan viewed a
powerless church interspersed with his own devices. God is
again calling His people to holiness and when the warning is
again given, it shall be followed by a triumphant church moving
in the authority of their commander, conquering and going
forth to conquer, being protected by the voice of the Holy Spirit
as He warns, "Touch not mine anointed."

*And Mordecai went out from the presence of the
king in royal apparel of blue and white, and with a
great crown of gold, and with a garment of fine
linen and purple; and the city of Shushan rejoiced
and was glad. (8:15)*

A royal spirit in a royal family crowned with glory and power
transforms a once-perplexed city from one of confusion to a city
of rejoicing. When the Holy Spirit possesses us, it demands
mixture to depart and enables us to make a difference in our
surroundings because of His presence in us.

*The Jews had light, and gladness, and joy and
honour.
And in every province, and in every city, whithersoever the king's commandment and his decree
came, the Jews had joy and gladness, a feast and
a good day. And many of the people of the land*

became Jews; for the fear of the Jews fell upon them. (8:16,17)

When mixture and confusion have been abolished, when we have been freed to war and win, then is light restored. Too many of us have been satisfied with the light of yesterday with no understanding that the path of the just is one of increasing illumination.

It is only as we walk in the truth of past revelation that we are able to receive present revelation. This light is followed by gladness, joy, and honor. Understanding that, we no longer fear His guidance but anticipate it by immediate appropriation of that which He has shown us.

The true witness of the church is power and joy when they are prominently displayed in us, God's showcase. A reverence and hunger for our God cause many to become His followers.

Blessed Jesus, not only have You redeemed me, but You have restored to me all that I have allowed Satan and sin to take away. I praise You this day, for Your restorative power and I pray that You will not allow me to be content with only a portion of my inheritance. Stir me, O Lord of my Father, shake me from lethargy and challenge me with all the promises of Your Word. Provisionally I am complete in You, Jesus, and I claim the reality of that provision now, in Your name. You are my King and my Lord, and in Your power I live and love and minister. Blessed be the King. Amen.

XII

Voice of Victory

Esther 9

Now in the twelfth month, that is, the month of Adar, on the thirteenth day of the same, when the king's commandment and his decree drew near to be put in execution, in the day that the enemies of the Jews hoped to have power over them, (though it was turned to the contrary, that the Jews had rule over them that hated them;)

The Jews gathered themselves together in their cities throughout all the provinces of the king Ahasuerus, to lay hand on such as sought their hurt: and no man could withstand them; for the fear of them fell upon all people.

And all the rulers of the provinces, and the lieutenants, and the deputies, and officers of the king, helped the Jews; because the fear of Mordecai fell upon them.

For Mordecai was great in the king's house, and his fame went out throughout all the provinces: for this man Mordecai waxed greater and greater.

Thus the Jews smote all their enemies with the

stroke of the sword, and slaughter, and destruc-
tion, and did what they would unto those that
hated them. (9:1-5)

The hope of the enemy to rule the church of Jesus Christ is filled with hopelessness for the reverse has been decreed by the King. It is when the people of God gather together unto Him, allowing the Holy Spirit to wax greater and greater as they progressively move in the authority and the name of their King, that this decree is fulfilled. Partial victory is no longer acceptable, thus the Jews smote all of their enemies.

And the king said unto Esther the queen, The
Jews have slain and destroyed five hundred men
in Shushan the palace, and the ten sons of
Haman; what have they done in the rest of the
king's provinces? now what is thy petiton? and it
shall be granted thee: or what is thy request further?
and it shall be done. (9:12)

As the king recounts with Esther the victories of warfare, we once again see the importance of progressing in prayer. It is the king who asks her for her petition and promises its fulfillment. No hesitation do we see in Esther for she knows what needs to be done, yet even in that knowledge, a higher goal than present victory is evident in her words, "If it please the king."

Then said Esther, If it please the king, let it be
granted to the Jews which are in Shushan to do to
morrow also according unto this day's decree,
and let Haman's ten sons be hanged upon the
gallows.

> *And the king commanded it so to be done: and the decree was given at Shushan; and they hanged Haman's ten sons.*
> *For the Jews that were in Shushan gathered themselves together on the fourteenth day also of the month Adar, and slew three hundred men at Shushan; but on the prey they laid not their hands. (9:13-15)*

The request that Haman's ten sons be hanged on the gallows is not made in a lack of mercy, rather in the maturity that realizes that that which has been destroyed yet lives in a new generation which has been steeped in the ways and concepts of the enemy.

Hatred, irreverence, and animosity toward God have set the goal for the destruction of His followers. Unless they, too, are eliminated, the battle will continue and the war will not be won. That the ultimate intention of the request was to establish a kingdom that pleased the king is further evidenced in that they took none of the prey. While we may share in His victory, we may not take the glory.

> *But the other Jews that were in the king's provinces gathered themselves together, and stood for their lives, and had rest from their enemies, and slew of their foes seventy and five thousand, but they laid not their hands on the prey. (9:16)*

Some are in the front battling. Some are just breathing in and out. Remember the story of the man who hired laborers for a penny a day? He hired some the last hour and gave them a penny and those that worked all day said, "Unfair, unfair; we worked all day for that which they got for one hour."

The master said, "So? I hired you for a penny a day. I hired them for a penny an hour. What is unfair?"

Why is it that some people seem to have it so easy in life and get so blessed? And others just scratch and scrape enduring trial after trial, and problem after problem. The answer is those who go through trials have grace to go through trials. They have the courage and strength to come out of it, or God would never have let them go through it. But those who don't go through it, don't need it or can't make it through. The important thing is not whether we are on the front lines; rather it is whether or not we please the King, for when we do, we are a blessing to all and a part of the victory.

> On the thirteenth day of the month Adar; and on
> the fourteenth day of the same rested they, and
> made it a day of feasting and gladness. (9:17)

How did it become a day? They made it a day of feasting and gladness. Every day we have that choice. It could be a day of doom and gloom or feasting and gladness. We set the tone when we get out of bed, or before. When we begin to sing in our spirits, "This is the day." probably one percent of us feel like starting the day that way. But everyone who will, makes it a day of feasting and gladness. We make it a day of feasting by appropriating the meat of maturity in everything that happens in the day.

> But the Jews that were at Shushan assembled
> together on the thirteenth day thereof, and on the
> fourteenth thereof; and on the fifteenth day of the
> same they rested, and made it a day of feasting

and gladness.

Therefore the Jews of the villages, that dwelt in the unwalled towns, made the fourteenth day of the month Adar a day of gladness and feasting, and a good day, and of sending portions to one another. (9:18,19)

Clearly we see a fulfillment of Colossians 3:15, "And let the peace of God rule in your hearts, to the which also ye are called in one body; and be ye thankful." All the Jews have come together under the rule of the king and are peacefully rejoicing. There is a vast difference between bragging and being thankful. Too many of our victories are followed by endless words describing every detail of our involvement in the success. We teach others our formulas and battle strategy rather than pointing them to the source of our victory. Knowing that such boasting displaces God as Lord, in our lives, we are instructed to give thanks in all things for it is in doing this that our eyes remain fixed on Him who has given the victory.

Thanksgiving then serves not to satisfy the needs of an egomaniac, but rather to equip a warrior for the next battle and the next victory.

And Mordecai wrote these things, and sent letters unto all the Jews that were in all the provinces of the king Ahasuerus, both nigh and far,

To stablish this among them, that they should keep the fourteenth day of the month Adar, and the fifteenth day of the same, yearly,

As the days wherein the Jews rested from their enemies, and the month which was turned unto them from sorrow to joy, (9:20-22a)

111

Purim was established as a time of remembering victory. We are never just delivered from the enemy, but always delivered unto the King; never just from sin, but unto abundant life. Mordecai established this day of remembrance. How important it is for us to allow the Holy Spirit to bring to our remembrance the victories we have experienced. It is in the expression of gratitude and praise to God that faith is stirred for new victories ahead.

> *from sorrow to joy, and from mourning into a good day: that they should make them days of feasting and joy, and of sending portions one to another, and gifts to the poor. (9:22a)*

The sharing of that gladness is seen as they send portions one to another. Paul said in 1 Corinthians 11:23, "For I have received of the Lord that which also I have delivered unto you." Each victory of our lives is meant to be shared. It is most encouraging to hear the testimony of one who has experienced victory in an area in which we presently battle. This does not mean that we have no word of comfort for those battling in areas which are unfamiliar to us, for the Spirit of counsel indwells us.

> *The Jews ordained, and took upon them, and upon their seed, and upon all such as joined themselves unto them, so as it should not fail, that they would keep these two days according to their writing, and according to their appointed time every year;*
> *And that these days should be remembered and*

*kept throughout every generation, every family,
every province, and every city; and that these days
of Purim should not fail from among the Jews, nor
the memorial of them perish from their seed.
(9:27,28)*

Psalm 145:4 declares that one generation shall praise God's works and acts to another. It is possible that the failure to do this has resulted in our continuing need to pray, "Thy kingdom come." When revelation and God's victories are buried with one generation, it demands that the new generation can only be prepared to receive the same revelation and little else. Purim was established as a reminder for the generations that were to follow that deliverance and gladness come only from the king. We must not fail to teach the principles of the kingdom and the necessity of the presence of the King to all who follow us.

*Then Esther the queen, the daughter of Abihail,
and Mordecai the Jew, wrote with all authority, to
confirm the second letter of Purim. (9:29)*

It is significant that Esther, by the authority of the king, is writing to confirm that which Mordecai has established. In the mouth of two or more witnesses is the word established. It is when the words that the church speaks are in agreement with the Holy Spirit that they become words of peace and truth. It will be when the Spirit and the bride say "Come," that the last victory will have been won for the last battle will have been fought and we shall rest at last in eternal victory.

113

God of All Battles, You are the God of all victories. Forgive me for so focusing my sight on the negative that I fail to delight in the positive victory which You have afforded me. Teach me to be thankful. Let Your Holy Spirit remind me of that which I have to be thankful for. O Father, grant that my influence shall always be used to encourage others to live a life of thanksgiving, for in the giving of thanks is faith nurtured, without which it is impossible to please the King. My thankful heart says, Amen.

XIII

Worship His Majesty

Esther 10

And the king Ahasuerus laid a tribute upon the land, and upon the isles of the sea.

And all the acts of his power and of his might, and the declaration of the greatness of Mordecai, whereunto the king advanced him, are they not written in the book of the chronicles of the kings of Media and Persia?

For Mordecai the Jew was next unto king Ahasuerus, and great among the Jews, and accepted of the multitude of his brethren, seeking the wealth of his people, and speaking peace to all his seed. (10:1-3)

What is Mordecai's purpose? The welfare of his people. May we never lose sight of the fact that the Holy Spirit is out to do us good seeking our maturity, prosperity, and welfare that we may be pleasing to the King. To this He has been promoted.

Someone is missing in chapter 10. Esther is gone. Fifty-five times throughout this glorious book, Esther's name is mentioned, either as the myrtle, Hadassah, or Esther the hidden, or Esther the star. Suddenly in the end, no Esther. She has become lost in Him. Poems and songs and sayings have been written about hiding behind the cross and hiding in Jesus, but how quickly we rush out to be seen. Esther does what she is bidden to do, moves into a totally successful ministry, and then steps back behind the Holy Spirit pointing to the King and saying, "All glory and honor and power and might and majesty be unto Thee, O God, and to thy Christ both now and forever."

O King Eternal and Lover of My Soul, I long to be so lost in You that self-goals need no longer be ignored as I accept Your promise that when I so delight in You, the desires of my heart are granted. With all my heart, soul, and being, I both fall and stand before You, and engulfed in Your love, I worship Your Majesty. Amen.

Notes:

Notes:

Notes:

Notes:

Notes:

IVERNA TOMPKINS MINISTRY, INC.
2945 PHEASANT DRIVE
DECATUR, GA 30034

(Postpaid Prices)

☐ GOD AND I $5.95
☐ HOW TO BE HAPPY IN NO MAN'S LAND $5.95
☐ HOW TO LIVE WITH KIDS AND ENJOY IT $5.95
☐ IF IT PLEASE THE KING .... *NEW* . $5.95
☐ SEVEN STEPS TO WORSHIP *(Booklet)* $1.50
☐ THE HOLY AND THE PROFANE *(Booklet)* $1.50
☐ THE RAVISHED HEART .... *NEW* . $5.95
☐ THE WAY TO HAPPINESS $3.50
☐ THE WORTH OF A WOMAN.................... $5.95

Available at your local bookstore or use this handy coupon:

Please send me the books I have checked above. I am
enclosing $_____ (Postpaid). Please
send check or money order.

Name _____

Address _____

City _____ State _____

Zip _____